ROMANTIC
FRENCH HOMES

ROMANTIC
FRENCH HOMES

LANIE GOODMAN

photography by **Simon Brown**

CICO BOOKS

LONDON NEW YORK

Published in 2013 by CICO Books
An imprint of
Ryland Peters & Small
20–21 Jockey's Fields
London WC1R 4BW

519 Broadway, 5th Floor
New York, NY 10012

10 9 8 7 6 5 4 3 2 1

Text, design, and photography © CICO Books
2013

A CIP catalog record for this book is available
from the Library of Congress and the British
Library.

ISBN: 978 1 908862 76 1

Printed in China

Editor: Gillian Haslam
Designer: Paul Tilby
Photographer: Simon Brown

CONTENTS

INTRODUCTION

"Romanticism is precisely situated neither in choice of subject nor exact truth, but in the way of feeling," wrote French *fin-de-siècle* poet Charles Baudelaire, who redefines "romantic" in terms of intimacy, spirituality, and color.

This elusory feeling of vibrant emotion evoked by Baudelaire is one of the most distinctive features of French interiors. Conceived as livable works of art, the atmosphere and décor of French homes reflect a certain insouciance for rules. Beyond the search for elegance and comfort, there's something intangible—call it *fantaisie*, whimsy—that shapes the soul of each house.

This book takes readers on an unprecedented journey from the honey-colored stone bastides and village houses of the sunlit Côte d'Azur, Provence, and Languedoc Roussillon, up across the Alps, and to secret corners of Paris and grand Norman castles.

These fourteen exceptional private homes include the former country retreats of illustrious Frenchmen—Alexis de Tocqueville, Louis Renault, and Marcel Pagnol. Whether a majestic country estate or a humble beach cottage, the memory-imbued walls continue to inspire the owners of today.

Likewise, among the many expatriate artists who settled in France, American *Vogue* photographer Henry Clark and Dutch turn-of-the-century painter Philip Zilcken are represented here. Their homes are resplendent examples of peaceful havens on the Riviera that were given a new life.

France's numerous Mediterranean influences—ancient Greek, Roman, or Italian—are also present in the interiors, a cultural cross-pollination of styles. Inseparable from every décor is an open window onto the exterior—a patch of burnished blue sea, the shimmering reflections of a river, a leafy vineyard, a lush flower garden, a snowy Alpine peak, or an iconic Parisian cathedral.

Above all, what these houses all share is their personalized theatrical *mise-en-scène*, a harmonious assemblage of colors, materials, and textures that actively re-invent the essence of romantic reveries.

ABOVE: **Flower gardens and an early seventeenth-century dovecote with 2000 putlogs at the Château d'Outrelaise in Normandy.**

OPPOSITE: **A corner of a bedroom at the Villa Baulieu, a restored Italianate-Provençal castle in the south of France. The Louis XVI-style canopy bed and rare eighteenth-century "deux pigeons" wallpaper were part of the original furnishings of the country mansion, whose former residents included numerous Counts of Provence and notable aristocrats.**

CHÂTEAUX

The traditional style of Norman castles dates back to medieval times when William the Conqueror, who invaded and took England in the eleventh century, built his own strategically located fortified château in the coastal city of Caen. Throughout the centuries, these aristocratic country dwellings were expanded and rebuilt, creating a hybrid of different styles that featured donjons, crenelated towers, dovecotes, belvederes, and vaulted carriage houses. During the early twentieth century, in the spirit of these grand family homes, renowned French automaker Louis Renault designed and built his own version of a rural riverside castle, transforming his 4200-acre "fiefdom" into a thriving agricultural mini-village.

OPPOSITE: The timeless river view from the main living room. The decorative terra-cotta fruit and flowers and original drop-leaf antique chandelier once belonged to the Renault family. A view of the exterior of the Art-Deco pool house. Detail of a marble chimneypiece. The majestic oak stairwell and a light fixture chosen by Renault. The automaker's boathouse, constructed in 1906, used to store his numerous yachts and sailboats.

RIGHT: The park view of the Château de la Batellerie, a Norman-style Verona stone and brick manor house, custom-designed for Louis Renault by the well-known Parisian architect André-Louis Arfvidson, completed in 1909.

Glimpsed from the Seine, the Château de la Batellerie, a nineteenth-century Anglo-Norman-style stone manor house, perched on a grassy riverbank, so impressed its former owner that he decided to buy it on sight.

CHÂTEAU DE LA BATELLERIE
HERQUEVILLE

The legendary anecdote, recounted in several biographies, began one summer's day in 1905 when famed French automaker Louis Renault was returning from Le Havre on his 60-foot yacht with his beloved opera-singer mistress, Jeanne Hatto. Cruising around a bend in the Seine, he saw that the small manor house and surrounding land were for sale. The romantic pastoral location struck him as ideal, midway between city and sea. In this sleepy agricultural village of Herqueville, some 80 miles north of Paris, near Rouen, Renault visualized a secluded romantic weekend refuge where he could moor his yacht and come and go as he pleased, far from the pressures of his factories. Known for his iron-willed determination, the industrialist set about purchasing the property along with two adjacent farms, and allegedly returned to Paris that evening with a bill of sale in his pocket. Through skilled negotiations with the Mayor's office, Renault would later acquire three other farms, their surrounding property, and a tiny ancient chapel.

Today, this carefully preserved three-story home, the main house of Renault's sprawling 4200-acre estate that once included a ten-bedroom guest annex, an Art-Deco pool, and five farms, is owned by David Salamone. A racecar enthusiast, retired movie stunt driver, and fashion photographer, he bought the Château de la Batellerie in 1999. Despite the stunning views of the Seine, there were some definite drawbacks.

"When I came here, it had been abandoned for nearly 40 years and it was in ruins," David recalls. "Water was running down the walls and I needed to replace the electricity and plumbing. It took me two years to restore it, with men working here day and night."

To fully appreciate the distinctive character of his home, the owner says he has amassed a collection of books, rare archives, and vintage photos of Louis Renault and his family at Herqueville, now on display in his library.

Back in 1906, the Château de la Batellerie, an eclectic mix of Gothic, Moorish, and Norman architecture, was entirely rebuilt and redesigned by Renault's favorite architect, André-Louis Arfvidson to accommodate the automaker's needs and the endless stream of weekend guests. In the early days, these included well-known political figures of the Belle Epoque, from Aristide Briand to the future French President, Raymond Poincaré. Lavish dinners were served in the formal dining room or on the glassed-in veranda overlooking the Seine, always accompanied by the finest vintages from Renault's vast wine cellar. Jeanne Hatto's illustrious artistic circle included composers Gabriel Fauré and Maurice Ravel, who were apparently bewildered by Renault's dubious taste in practical jokes at Herqueville dinner parties. He would pierce holes in his guests' wine glasses, "inadvertently" drop a chocolate cream dessert into a young lady's décolleté, or put a garden snake in a guest's bed.

The ground floor also included a reception room, a Louis XV-style salon, and the spacious dining

Guests included composers Gabriel Fauré and Maurice Ravel, writer Antoine de Saint-Exupéry, statesman Aristide Briand, and the King of Spain, Alfonso XIII

ABOVE: The wood-paneled pantry and Renault's modern "telephone box" room behind the door.

OPPOSITE: The massive oak staircase is made from one single piece of wood. No details were overlooked, including the radiators, painted to match the carved panels. Hanging on the wall are photos by David Salamone.

room with an ornately sculpted fireplace, precious wood paneling, and antique crystal chandeliers. The monumental marble staircase leads to the two upper floors with spacious bedrooms and Art-Deco bathrooms. In those early days, the first floor was reserved for Renault's fiancée, Mademoiselle Hatto (who was later given her own home on the Herqueville property, remaining a life-long friend); the second-floor master bedroom was designated for "Monsieur Louis." Current owner David Salamone, who has kept the room in the spirit of its original country elegance and restored the bathrooms with the same vivid coral and green tiles chosen by Renault, now occupies it.

When Jeanne Hatto, who resented Renault's possessive beleaguering, finally refused to marry him, the industrialist courted a haughty, beautiful young woman, Christiane Bouillaire, who was the daughter of a notary. Soon after their wedding in the small Herqueville chapel in 1918, Christiane took on the role of the sparkling hostess at their country estate. Their formal dinners were always a mix of Parisian high society, famous writers such as Antoine de Saint-Exupéry and Pierre Drieu La Rochelle (of whom she became enamored, much to Louis' chagrin), and even foreign royalty such as the King of Spain, Alfonso XIII.

ABOVE LEFT: The whitewashed walls were given a fresh coat of paint, but date back to Renault's own predilection for simplicity. The wood table was found in India during the present owner's travels.

ABOVE RIGHT: The dining room is furnished with a restored 1901 library table that was originally from the Blixen castle in Africa. The antique chimneypiece was brought in by Renault, most probably retrieved from a nearby castle.

OPPOSITE: The music room. The elaborate wooden double doors and exposed rustic beams date to the Château's construction, which took two full years to complete under Renault's vigilant supervision. The sofa is from George Smith, London. The bookcases against the wall contain original rare documents; the architect's drawings for the construction of the Château de la Batellerie are on display on the back wall.

OPPOSITE: The study/working room, furnished with Knoll leather armchairs and a Persian carpet. On the carved oak mantelpiece is an antique Indian dowry box. The custom-designed drawers were used to store Renault's plans and documents.

ABOVE: Louis Renault, an ingenious "tinker," designed his own meticulously stenciled tool cabinets in his workroom to keep every wrench and screwdriver in order. The owner has preserved all Renault's original antique drop-leaf crystal chandeliers.

family garden shed; aged nine, he invented a small camera, installed electricity at his home when no one else had it , and later designed his first steam-run car tricycle at the age of 21.

By the time Renault purchased his home in Herqueville, seven years later, the mass production of his cars at the Billancourt factories had begun to soar, rivaling Citroën and Peugeot, with 45 types of cars and employing 8,000 workers. Yet, beyond Renault's two main passions—cars and yachting—he had a peasant's love of the earth, stones, and land. His grandfather had come from generations of winemakers from the Loire valley, and in the château wine cellar, David Salamone says he found a few dusty bottles that are "precious relics" from Renault's collection of prize vintages and remain untouched.

In later years, Renault constantly sought to improve every acre he owned. The property was in perpetual transformation, particularly from 1910 to 1934, when he tried to develop the domain into an agricultural utopia. Having little tolerance for waste of any kind, the industrialist made use of his extensive apple orchard by creating a cider brewery, and even started a bee farm to produce honey. The Herqueville interiors were always filled with hydrangeas from the garden, where the Renaults' only son, Jean-Louis, used to play.

While restoring Renault's home to its former glory, David says he was astounded by the number of modern comforts that Renault had anticipated, from double-glazed windows to strategically placed radiators in the corridor leading to the black and gold tiled Deco heated pool. "Many of the rugs and wall hangings were missing, but Renault's original chandeliers—which were probably quite expensive for a country 'cottage'—were still intact," he says. Perhaps the most surprising feature of the château is Louis' "work room" on the ground floor, with custom-made, meticulously stenciled tool cabinets to keep every wrench or screwdriver in order. They are still in mint condition. "As early as the 1920s, Renault

A self-made man, mechanical genius, and inventor, Renault's colossal industrial enterprise made him not only famous but one of the wealthiest men of his era. In those years, he was considered "the Henry Ford of France;" today he might have been compared to the visionary ingenuity of Bill Gates. As a child, he was always tinkering with machines and engines in the

Christiane Bouillaire, the daughter of a notary, and Louis Renault were wed in the small Herqueville chapel in 1918, where they are now buried

also devised a gadget that could change ten records at a time on the gramophone," says David.

Carved into the wood beams of the veranda is another reminder of Renault's life at Herqueville—a sculpted relief of Marcel Renault, Louis' younger brother, who died in 1903 in a car crash during a competitive race. Among the more amusing structural oddities of Château de la Batellerie is the maze of underground passageways built by Renault so that the staff could pass unseen through the house.

Awarded the highest status of the French Legion of Honor after the First World War, Renault was later accused of collaborating with the Nazis and fabricating tanks for the Germans during the Second World War. He died without a trial under mysterious circumstances in prison in October 1944 at the age of 67, written out of French history books.

His monumental empire was confiscated and nationalized by De Gaulle's provisional government in 1945. Today his eight grandchildren, who have initiated legal action against the French State to seek compensation and restore Renault's reputation, have challenged that decision.

Louis and Christiane are buried in front of the tiny chapel of Herqueville where they were married. "Every man wants to leave four things behind him before he disappears: the house he built, the tree he planted, the book he wrote, and the son he engendered," Renault was once quoted as saying. Fortunately, Renault's cherished home, the Château de la Batellerie, has been given a new life. "At the height of Herqueville, Renault had 42 gardeners. Today, I have one," says David. "Still, even the trees he planted are carefully tended."

OPPOSITE LEFT: The antique Arabian wall painting was part of the original décor of Christiane Renault's bedroom and restored by the owner.

OPPOSITE RIGHT AND THIS PAGE: Formerly the bedroom of the maîtresse de maison, Madame Renault. The owner visited the local brocante for many of the furnishings, including the bed stand and dressing table. The original moldings, decorative columns, some of the curtains, and the Versailles parquet floors all date back to the turn of the century.

ABOVE: A view of the castle and its gardens. The Château d'Outrelaise, originally built in 1534 by Gaspard Le Marchant, a brilliant royal jurist and royal counselor, was continually extended and transformed up until the nineteenth century. The property includes two Neo-Renaissance avant-corps, an arched postern gatehouse, and a vast dovecote.

OPPOSITE: The dovecote and main entrance door, built in 1894. The music room; inscribed above the carved marble chimneypiece, dated 1584: "Quieti, Amicis, Posteris." A guest bedroom lined with wallpaper that the owners pieced together from a jeweler's old ledger of bills. An engraving of Queen Victoria hangs above a handcrafted wooden table. The small circular domed sixteenth-century belvedere is still accessible today.

CHÂTEAU D'OUTRELAISE
NORMANDY

At the majestic entrance of the Château d'Outrelaise stands a sixteenth-century graceful statue of two Roman deities: Vertumnus, god of seasons and change, and Pomona, a wood nymph. It was sculpted by the Norman "Leonardo di Vinci" of the era, Marin Le Bourgeoys, whose rendition of Ovid's mythological lovers couldn't be more emblematic of the spirit of this ancient castle. Situated twelve miles from Caen, the château and surrounding property have all been restored by its current owners to evoke the gentle grandeur of its rich history.

The lush 75-acre park is particularly noteworthy because of its vast variety of styles, a mix of formal French and English gardens and a wild pastoral landscape. Rows of aligned century-old plane trees lead through the arched postern gate and Renaissance-style pavilion to the twenty-room, L-shaped main house, crowned with a small, domed sixteenth-century belvedere. The extensive grounds, which are open to the public in the summer by appointment, provide a glimpse of the castle's waterfalls, stone bridges, flower gardens, fruit orchards, and grassy meadows. Outrelaise derives its name from its geographical location—a path through woods leads to the Laize River, and the castle is literally "on the other side" of the riverbank.

ABOVE LEFT AND ABOVE RIGHT: The entrance hall, lined with artwork. A copy of a bust attributed to Raphael from a wax mold. The original hangs in the Musée de Lille. Detail of an angel and ornamentation from numerous chimneypieces in the château.

OPPOSITE: The impressive wrought-iron banister was crafted in the eighteenth century, signed by Roche. Below the stairs, an eighteenth-century Provençal small table adorned with peonies plucked from the owners' garden.

As in similar properties throughout the region, the progressive transformation of the château spanned from the sixteenth century to the nineteenth century. Parisian architect Rémy du Rosel, who was said to have been inspired by his former construction of the elegant layout of the Place des Vosges, laid down the first bricks and stones of the seventeenth-century wing in 1604.

Son of wealthy silk merchant Jean Le Marchant, the castle's aristocratic first owner, Gaspard Le Marchant, served as the royal counsellor of Henri III and Henri IV. Known as a man of taste and culture and a brilliant jurist, Gaspard Le Marchant had no heirs and the castle was bequeathed to his nephew, Jacques Blondel de Tilly, the first of numerous successions. By the eighteenth century, under

ABOVE AND RIGHT: A workspace corner of the music room, furnished with a variety of antique pieces: the desk chair dates from the Louis XIII era. From the owners' collection of glass spheres.

OPPOSITE: The present owners opted to keep the original nineteenth-century wood paneled interiors and exposed beam ceilings in the music room/library. The fireplace is a cozy spot for tea and after-dinner digestifs. The turn-of-the-century player piano still cranks out tunes from the era.

the Polignac family, the main house had been extended to include a large wing to the right, flanked by two imposing Neo-Renaissance avant-corps, and an impressive seventeenth-century dovecote with 2000 putlogs, whose domed tiled roof was unfortunately destroyed during the Second World War.

The present owners, who work in decoration, graphics, and design, acquired Château d'Outrelaise in 1989. The castle had weathered well, despite the intermittent vacant periods between the arrival and departure of its former residents. "The walls of the buildings were still in good condition," the owners explain. "We had to replace all the electrical wiring, but the biggest challenge was cleaning and landscaping the park and gardens." Over the last two decades, Jean-Louis and Walid have gradually refurbished the main house, room by room, adding modern touches to create a sense of balance with the antique furnishings and ornate woodwork. But the charm of Outrelaise lies

"The general feel to the room is in the spirit of eighteenth-century Louis XV. Most of all, we wanted simplicity."

not only in its decoration but also in the contrast of colors, textures, and styles. "Most of the objects are from a personal collection of what the French call *coups de cœur*—something you fall in love with at first sight—picked up in auctions, from antique dealers, or during my travels," says Jean-Louis. Nearest to the entrance hall, the luminous ground-floor salon is a perfect example of the art of combining new and old. Originally lined with eighteenth-century-style somber polished wood paneling, the walls were stripped and painted over in white. "The furniture is Provincial Italian, which we also whitewashed, but the general feel to the room is in the spirit of

ABOVE AND ABOVE RIGHT: A pair of eighteenth-century Louis XV French Provençal armchairs. The legs and armrests were painted white to create a touch of modernity.

RIGHT AND OPPOSITE: The twenty-room castle's sunny whitewashed salon blanc combines family heirlooms with a contemporary light fixture in iron and paper and a 1920s Tunisian rug. The blue-and-white reupholstered daybed from the Louis XV era is one of many restored family pieces.

eighteenth-century Louis XV. Most of all, we wanted simplicity." Instead of a leaf drop crystal chandelier, the owner opted for a hanging modern light fixture of their own creation, made of cream and white paper. They also chose a pretty patterned Tunisian rug to create warmth.

In the adjacent wood-paneled library, the highlight is the century-old player piano—a gift from friends—that came with a huge collection of perforated music. One of the most striking features of the room is the tall, white stone sixteenth-century multicolored marble

chimneypiece that had been meticulously restored by previous owners. "We often have tea or after-dinner drinks here on winter nights in front of the fireplace," Jean-Louis says.

Formal dinners are held in the dining room, lined with antique family portraits that date back to Louis XIII and the seventeenth century. During the refurbishment, the owners decided to strip away the overly ornate nineteenth-century-style dark wood paneling to brighten the room. Another change to recapture the château's original sixteenth-century character was to remove the over-

OPPOSITE: The formal dining room retains its country atmosphere by adding nineteenth-century painted iron garden chairs. The castle's overly ornate chimneypiece was replaced with a new design to recapture the castle's original sixteenth-century clean simple lines. A seventeenth-century oil painting from the owners' family collection.

ABOVE AND LEFT: Flowers, including peonies and rare old roses, picked from the garden, the owners' pride and joy. The country kitchen is the hub of social gatherings. The owners salvaged a wooden farm table and church chairs from antique markets. In the alcove: an antique iron urn mounted on the remains of an eighteenth-century faux-marble fountain.

elaborate chimney and replace it with a simpler fireplace of their own design, inspired by the clean sharp lines of those at the Château d'Ecouen in the Val d'Oise, near Paris.

Most of the dining takes place in the spacious, spare country kitchen, where the owners linger over meals with friends. The choice of straight-back cane chairs and a long wooden antique table is in the same quest for authenticity, says the owner, as is a collection of old bottles. The pantry is stocked with homemade jams, chutneys, pickles, and beans, all plucked from the fruit orchards and carefully tended vegetable patch. "We spend a great deal of time cooking," Walid recounts, "and many of the ingredients are all just within arm's reach."

One key feature of the château gardens—the owners' pride and joy—is the glorious bed of peonies cultivated in every shade of pink. Another section is devoted to a variety of old roses from eras gone by.

OPPOSITE FAR LEFT AND LEFT: The owners chose to furnish all of the bedrooms with stone-tiled floors and hand-stitched Provençal boutis bedspreads, and paint the walls in bright shades of blue and yellow to add a more contemporary touch to the upper stories. Hanging from the closet is an antique vest from the Louis XV era. The oil paintings in the bathroom are part of a series by Bernadette Kelly.

ABOVE LEFT AND RIGHT: The spacious master bedroom, named "La Chambre Royale." One of many Delft vases and garden flowers brighten up the room.

On the first and second floors of the castle, the owners decided on a more whimsical color scheme for their five guest bedrooms, adding two-tone stripes on the ceilings where one would expect to see exposed wood beams. The larger rooms were painted in a medley of sky blue and mauve; warm ochers and reds were chosen in smaller attic rooms that once served for the staff. In the master bedroom, Jean-Louis says he strove for a rustic simplicity—stripped wood floors, antique quilted *boutis* on the beds, a few cherished family furnishings, and a series of works by Bernadette Kelly, who was Jean-Louis' painting teacher, and Belgian artist Marcel Delmotte.

"We often have guests who are professional photographers and interested in shooting fashion catalogs here," says the owner. "As a decorator, you have to adapt. I love what the past centuries can offer, but I also like color and fantasy." No wonder the Château d'Outrelaise has remained one of the most inviting castles in Normandy, but that is apparently an age-old reputation. Engraved in gold letters on black marble on the ancient door that led pedestrians to the exit is the following: *"Qui veut se tenir à son aise ne doit pas sortir Outrelaise."* Those who seek comfort should not go any further than Outrelaise.

"I love what the past centuries can offer, but I also like color and fantasy," says Jean-Louis

LEFT: The "Patchwork" guest room under the eaves, lined with recycled paper. The chimney dates to the end of the eighteenth century.

ABOVE AND OPPOSITE: The rustic-style "Norwegian" bathroom, named for its Norwegian pine walls, with a nineteenth-century claw foot bathtub.

THIS PAGE: On the first and second floors, each of the five guest bedrooms are different, furnished with stone-tiled floors, nineteenth-century-style bathtubs, hand-stitched Provençal bedspreads, and rustic finds from the local antique stores.

OPPOSITE: The whimsical "Chambre des Factures," lined with antique ledger paper of a jeweler's bills, includes one of many wood bed stands designed by the owners.

"This place pleases me. I am going to lead an extremely regulated and peaceful life here," wrote Alexis de Tocqueville, the famed nineteenth-century author of "Democracy in America," philosopher, and politician, referring to his ancestral country château. Situated on Normandy's Cotentin peninsula, near Cherbourg, this graceful stone castle has been carefully preserved over the past century by several generations of Alexis de Tocqueville's descendants.

CHÂTEAU DE TOCQUEVILLE
NORMANDY

Now classified as a historic monument, the château has remained a joyful family home and a tranquil refuge from the urban bustle of Paris, in the spirit of Alexis de Tocqueville's beloved pastoral retreat. The most recent refurbishment was undertaken by the current owners, the Count and Countess de Tocqueville d'Hérouville, who spent two and a half years restoring the castle's Neo-Renaissance nineteenth-century square pavilion, transforming the space into an elegant three-story guest wing with five spacious bedrooms.

Surrounded by a verdant pasture, a forest of red oaks, and a vast English-style park (replete with a pond and a resident gliding white

OPPOSITE: The Château de Tocqueville, set in a lush 15-acre English-style garden park, is the ancestral home of the famed intellectual Alexis de Tocqueville (1805–1859), author of "Democracy in America." Originally a manor house in the sixteenth century, the castle was modified in the eighteenth and nineteenth centuries, and beautifully restored by the descendants of the Tocqueville family. Alexis de Tocqueville and his wife Mary replaced the once-shabby courtyard and formal clipped hedges with green lawns and a large pond.

FAR LEFT: Count Christian de Tocqueville, who lived on the estate, added the square pavilion in 1893. In the summer of 2012 the Count and Countess de Tocqueville d'Hérouville refurbished this entire wing, which includes five bedrooms, an elevator, and a modernized kitchen, .

LEFT: The sixteenth-century carriage house.

ABOVE: The rear stairway of the main tower. The door leads to a small chapel.

LEFT: The Count and Countess Guy and Marie-Henriette d'Hérouville were behind the meticulous twenty-year restoration of the salons after the devastating accidental fire of 1954, when the ground floor of the castle was partially destroyed. No detail was overlooked to recapture the original eighteenth-century salon atmosphere, such as the Fragonard-style fresco of the countryside, painted above the doorway. Jean-Guillaume's mother, Marie-Henriette, chose the fabrics and made all the curtains.

BELOW: On the wall hangs a painting of a country picnic in Auvergne, portraying members of the Puy Ségur branch of the family ancestry.

OPPOSITE: The walls of the two summer living rooms were whitewashed and family pieces were brought in to replace the furnishings that were destroyed in the fire. Above the doorway is a painted landscape of the nearby port of Barfleur, where the Duke of Normandy set sail to conquer England in 1066.

swan), the striking composite style of the Château de Tocqueville is a reflection of the château's rich eventful past.

During the sixteenth century, the relatively modest estate was little more than a squat stone manor house flanked by two conical-roofed towers, with dormer windows, chimney stacks, and a rust-colored thatched straw roof, typical of the local architecture. Across the courtyard was a third monumental tower that served as a dovecote, with 2,500 niches and a single circular band of stone at its top. Significantly, this architectural feature of the dovecote also symbolized the ruling status of the landowner, whose power extended to a kind of justice of the peace. The château's majestic carriage house with a triple arcade also dates back to this period.

The family history begins in 1661, when the Clérel family acquired the manor and, according to custom, changed their name to the fief of their seigneury, Clérel de Tocqueville.

"During the French Revolution, there was no major damage to the property because the family had a good relationship with the peasants," explains Jean-Guillaume de Tocqueville d'Hérouville (the great-great-great-grand-nephew of Alexis de Tocqueville), who, like his wife, Stéphanie, is thoroughly well versed in the castle's fascinating history. "The laborers destroyed the roof of the dovecote because it was a symbol of nobility but also because the pigeons were eating their crops. Those who could read stormed the family library, opened all the books, and crossed out the word 'king' whenever they saw it."

By the eighteenth century, as the Tocqueville family's prosperity augmented, the manor was given larger windows, qualifying it as a château. During the latter part of the century, a central pavilion with an ornamental triangular pediment with a double coat of arms of the Tocqueville and Damas-Crux families was added. The thatched straw was also replaced by a roof of shale schist, typical of the Val de Saire region.

Born in Paris in 1805, Charles-Alexis Clérel de Tocqueville, the distinguished free-thinking writer, came from a long lineage of nobility and famous leaders and

ABOVE LEFT: An eighteenth-century family piece adorned by hydrangeas, plucked from the château gardens.

ABOVE: An eighteenth-century needlepoint chair and stool in the sunlit summer living room, with a double east–west exposure.

OPPOSITE: A view of one of two adjacent salons that serve as summer living rooms, where the family gathers for afternoon tea or aperitifs. The eighteenth-century chairs were rescued from the fire and reupholstered. On the back wall hangs an oval portrait of the Marquise de Mailloc; on the left, a portrait of Alexis de Tocqueville as a young man.

The furnishings are period pieces retrieved from the attic, family heirlooms, and faithful reproductions

magistrates. His illustrious descendants include the military architect Vauban, as well as Chrétien-Guillaume de Malesherbes, the famous botanist and humanist who defended Louis XVI at his trial and was subsequently guillotined in 1894, during the Terror. As fate would have it, some of Malesherbes' family members were spared the scaffold: the future parents of Alexis, Malesherbes' 22-year-old granddaughter, Louise-Madeleine Le Pelletier de Rosanbo, and her young husband, Hervé de Tocqueville, were also imprisoned but escaped their death sentence with the fall of Robespierre.

Brought up in the château de Verneuil-sur-Seine, near Paris, along with his elder brothers, Hippolyte and Edouard, Alexis de Tocqueville would eventually inherit the family property in Normandy from his father in 1836. Though somewhat dilapidated, drafty, and damp, the castle's neglected state did little to deter the writer's enthusiasm

OPPOSITE: **Both summer living rooms are showcases for family portraits. Above the door is a painted landscape of Cherbourg.**

ABOVE TOP LEFT: **A bust of Alexis de Tocqueville's grandfather, Bernard de Tocqueville.**

ABOVE CENTER: **The salvaged reupholstered eighteenth-century chairs were part of the long restoration, modeled after old postcards and photos of the salons.**

ABOVE LEFT: **The room is dominated by a large painting of the seventeen-year-old Alexis at lessons with his father, Count Hervé de Tocqueville.**

ABOVE: **A late eighteenth-century tambour-front mahogany desk is one of many family pieces brought to the country estate from Paris.**

ABOVE: Alexis de Tocqueville's extensive library included a diversity of tomes on history, sociology, and philosophy. Alexis de Tocqueville was also a great admirer of many of his literary contemporaries, including George Sand, and was a childhood friend and relative of François-René de Chateaubriand, founder of Romanticism in French literature,.

LEFT: Alexis de Tocqueville's working library has been carefully preserved in its original state, including the writer's desk and plume. A portrait of French military architect, Vauban, who figures in the ancestral lineage, hangs above the eighteenth-century oak paneled walls and carved chimneypiece.

and presumed blood ties with the region, since his father, Hervé, claimed to have had a forebear who sailed with the Duke of Normandy to England in 1066. In Alexis de Tocqueville's correspondence to his wife, Mary Mottley—an Englishwoman who was neither an aristocrat, Catholic, nor wealthy—he also speaks glowingly of his "family's old hovel," its sweeping view from the tower "a long prairie terminating in the sea on the horizon."

"Alexis and his wife Mary had no children, but had a loving, intellectual relationship," says Jean-Guillaume. "When they took over the estate, they completely transformed the formal French-style park into an English-style grassy meadow with a pond, and replaced the muddy lanes with a wider carriageway." Tocqueville, who spent long hours at his desk in the study, also installed an extra pane of glass to the sash windows in the first-floor gallery to avoid hearing the crunch of gravel made by the carriages. Even today, Tocqueville's presence is almost palpable in the impressive wood-paneled eighteenth-century-style library, filled with his meticulously preserved collection of books and maps.

After Alexis de Tocqueville's death in 1859, the castle was abandoned for almost forty years until the next heir, Count Christian de Tocqueville (the grandson of Alexis' brother, Edouard), added a new wing on the southern facade of the château. Later, during the Second World War, the Germans occupied the estate but did little damage to the buildings. After the Liberation, Ernest Hemingway reportedly spent two nights at the Tocqueville castle while it was a country hospital for American troops. "Legend has it that Hemingway carved his initials near

ABOVE: The oak-paneled dining room with a bust of celebrated French chemist and philosopher, Antoine Lavoisier, guillotined in 1794.

LEFT: To cover the flame-damaged walls, the Count and Countess d'Hérouville lined the room with a bright Pierre Frey "Giverny" pattern fabric.

OPPOSITE: The country-style dining room is often used for large family gatherings. The most striking feature is the elaborate carved stone Renaissance chimneypiece that dates back to 1623, originally retrieved from a German palace. It portrays biblical scenes from the Judgment of Solomon and David and Goliath, and was formerly located in the nineteenth-century wing of the château.

ABOVE: The "Basoche" patterned bedroom in the newly restored nineteenth-century pavilion.

ABOVE CENTER: The current owners hunted down unusual ornamental pieces to match the period furniture. The ceramic parrot was found at an antique warehouse in Paris.

ABOVE RIGHT: All the artwork that hangs in the pavilion bedrooms was retrieved from the château attic and expertly restored. On the wall is a marquise from the Puy Ségur branch of the Tocqueville lineage.

OPPOSITE: Alexis de Tocqueville's original bed, still in mint condition.

the castle's doorway and carried off a sextant left behind by a German officer," recounts Jean-Guillaume. "His initials might still be there, but the wall is made of soft stone and now covered with ivy."

The castle's history was marred by a tragic incident in 1954, when a fire broke out, due to a worker's negligence, and ravaged the castle and grounds. Though much of the ground-floor furnishings and artwork was destroyed, not all

was lost. The winding circular stone steps that lead to the upper story resisted the flames and somewhat miraculously the fire stopped at the door of the library, which held all of Alexis de Tocqueville's original precious papers and manuscripts. (They have since been safely archived and microfilmed.)

"My grandfather and my parents were heartbroken, but decided to replace what had burned," says Jean-Guilluame, who recounts that it took twenty years to repair the damage, using old postcards and photos to re-create the eighteenth-century-style furniture, some of which was crafted by old-timer local artisans who were familiar with the château.

One work that did not survive was a large family portrait of Hervé and his son Alexis, during a lesson in the study. "My grandfather, Count Jean, was on a bus one day in Paris and saw a man who had just been to an art auction at Drouot, carrying a copy of the very same painting," says Jean-Guillaume. Astounded, Jean de Tocqueville swiftly negotiated a sale on the spot and went off with the canvas, which now hangs in the newly decorated guest wing.

Authenticity and modern comfort were both key factors in rethinking the space of the pavilion. Stéphanie and Jean-Guillaume de Tocqueville salvaged as much as they could

from the original period-piece furnishings from the attic, completing the bedrooms with family heirlooms, from carpets to antique tables, brought from Paris. "We hardly bought anything, except for some of the beds," says Stéphanie, who found eighteenth-century-style four-posters to match the rooms, but outfitted the bathrooms with simple contemporary showers and sinks. A mix of colorful Pierre Frey wallpaper and Nya Nordiska fabrics was also used to brighten up the bedrooms.

Alexis de Tocqueville is buried at the foot of the village church, down the road from the estate. His final days were spent in Cannes battling tuberculosis, but the mild climate did little to soothe his longing for Normandy. In a last letter to a friend, he wrote: "I know you will keep fond memories of the poor château at Tocqueville: it is a place that is foremost in my heart and I would prefer to live under its sky, sometimes so sadly gentle and at other times so stormy and terrible, than to breathe the most fragrant air of the universe on the shores of the bluest and calmest sea."

OPPOSITE: The bedroom of the late Count Guy d'Hérouville, whose long labor of love in restoring the fire-damaged château has played a vital part of the home's recent history.

LEFT: The small but luminous "Capucine" room, lined with toile de Jouy wallpaper.

ABOVE: The simple elegance of the period furniture characterizes the Château de Tocqueville's uncluttered authentic charm. To the right, on the wall hangs a childhood portrait of Jean Guillaume's grandfather, Count Jean de Tocqueville, whose poor health from breathing in gases during the battle of Verdun during the First World War prevented him from spending prolonged periods at his beloved family estate during winter.

BASTIDES

The word "bastide" formerly alluded to a perched medieval fortified town, but has now come to designate a rose or ocher-toned country mansion in southern France where Provençal gentry once made their homes. With sweeping countryside views and surrounded by verdant orchards and vineyards, the charm of even the most humble bastide was its proximity to nature. The productive farmland was often complemented by more refined expressions of vegetal beauty, such as flower gardens with stone fountains and wisteria-shaded walkways. The rough equivalent of country living in Alpine regions is the chalet; by the 1920s, this mountain-style farmhouse made from locally sourced wood was transformed into a fashionable model of ski resort refinement.

SAVOYARD FARM CHALET
MEGÈVE

In 1916, when the unconventional Baroness Noémie de Rothschild became disenchanted with the glamorous Swiss ski resort of St Moritz, she and her banker husband decided to build an exclusive alternative in the French Alps. As improbable as it must have seemed at the time, the Baroness chose a sleepy authentic Savoyard village that was sunny all day long and more accessible than Val d'Isère.

ABOVE: The chalet is nestled at the foot of a mountain slope. The recycled wood was scrubbed and lacquered to maintain its natural grain. The Alpine earthy theme contrasts with metallic objets d'art and a cristal de roche sculpture, to "add harmony and well-being" says the owner.

RIGHT: View of the dining room. Chalet "Hauteluce," built from old materials salvaged from dismantled Savoyard farmhouses. The welcoming entrance, constructed from century-old stone, is flanked by clay pots of lavender and firewood.

Though no one had then heard of Megève, an agricultural hamlet west of Chamonix-Mont-Blanc, this former leather tannery town with its fourteenth-century Gothic church and charming "chocolate box" village houses would become one of the most popular ski resorts in Europe by the 1950s. Frequent guests at the Baroness' sumptuous hotel, the Palace Mont d'Arbois, included everyone from crowned heads such as King Albert of Belgium and Queen Elizabeth II to high society and artistic celebrities such as Edith Piaf, Marcel Pagnol, Josephine Baker, and Rita Hayworth. Even Hollywood had

ABOVE LEFT AND RIGHT: On the wall hangs a large photograph of a snowy scene in the woods, purchased in a Moscow gallery. The silvered cow skin rugs add a warm note to the polished stone floors.

OPPOSITE: The central contemporary-style pine fireplace, designed by the owner, divides the living room in two. Displayed on the crocodile-skin table by Philipp Plein is a bronze circular sculpture by the artist Jakos.

BELOW: Dolce, the Jack Russell terrier.

"Decorating is like writing—you find yourself in front of a blank page and you have a story to tell, something coherent and natural. The mountain architecture in Savoie is so pronounced that you don't want to distract the eye with too many colors," says Jocelyne Sibuet

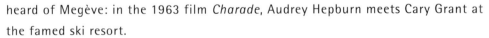

heard of Megève: in the 1963 film *Charade*, Audrey Hepburn meets Cary Grant at the famed ski resort.

Significantly, Megève is also the birthplace of the first contemporary-style ski chalet, thanks to the Baroness, who commissioned visionary French architect Henry Jacques le Même to build her personal home in 1929. Combining the traditional Savoyard farm with all the refined comforts of a *hôtel particulier*—a sloping roof and large balcony on the front facade with a streamlined Ruhlmann-inspired interior, Henry Jacques le Même would later create a veritable visual identity for Megève, designing over 200 chalets.

In the early 1980s, a young couple, Jocelyne and Jean-Louis Sibuet, followed in the footsteps of Megève's innovative sense of modernity when they bought and transformed a small slightly run-down chalet hotel, "Au Coin du Feu". But it was their next highly successful 1989 venture—"Les Fermes de Marie," nine sprawling luxurious interlinked chalets, a restaurant, and spa—that put Megève back on the map as a

ABOVE AND RIGHT: A bell jar containing pearly seashells, collected from the owner's travels. Authentic antlers hang on the walls.

OPPOSITE: In the dining room, a mix of old and new; a salvaged pine farm table, set off by Balthus chairs, a hanging glass light fixture, and Frey flannel curtains.

All the antlers were painted white "to transform a potentially kitsch local object into something beautiful," says the owner.

stylish destination for skiers. Since then, the ever-expanding Sibuet Hotels & Spa group, which now includes eight hotels scattered across the Alps, Lyon, and Provence, were all designed by Jocelyne Sibuet. Known for her distinctive mix of sleek contemporary lines, pale earthy hues, painted or bleached wood, richly textured fabrics, and original handpicked country antiques, the owner is now widely recognized as a pioneer of understated elegance in the hotel industry.

Her ongoing passion for decoration is "instinctive and self-trained," but nurtured by the tradition of her own roots. Born in the nearby Alpine village of Praz-sur-Arly, Jocelyne explains that her home, like her hotel design, was conceived as a harmonious, deeply comfortable "cocoon."

Her guiding principle, she says, is making use of locally sourced materials that will offset aspects of the regional architecture and the natural environment.

"Hauteluce," Jocelyne Sibuet's own two-story chalet, sits atop a quiet, winding country road, at the foot of a pine forest in the heights of Megève. Having scouted widely for salvaged old materials during the construction of "Les Fermes de Marie," Jocelyne and her former husband, Jean-Louis, decided to use their experience to build a spacious private home. Constructed in 2002 from a variety of recycled old timbers from neighboring dismantled farms, "every piece of wood was numbered, then reassembled," as Jocelyne explains. "The pine ceiling beams were never sanded or painted because the texture of the wood is so interesting. We just brushed them to bring out their natural color."

The ground-floor entrance leads up stairs to the vast luminous living room and dining room, a medley of soothing whites and muted grays with polished stone floors, deep sofas, and a centrally situated tall pine fireplace.

"I think that a home should create a kind of gentleness, as soon as you enter. It might start with a subtle play with the fabrics and materials, like soft wool and touches of fur that I put on the sofas and beds. I want to be surrounded by a peaceful

ABOVE LEFT: The heated indoor swimming pool with a view of the snowy slopes.

ABOVE: A small study, filled with family photos and books.

OPPOSITE: "A home should immediately feel soothing, comforting—like a cocoon—which is why I use flannel curtains and fur."

atmosphere, which is why I favor white. The mountain architecture in Savoie is so pronounced that you don't want to distract the eye with too many colors."

One manner of highlighting the Alpine surroundings was through meticulous attention to varied textures, which range from the silvered cow skin rugs, purchased in Belgium, to Frey curtains in creamy beige flannel or caramel suede. Jocelyne's sense of combination might include a few pearly seashells under a glass bell, an abstract bronze sculpture by the artist Jako,

Conviviality is a key feature, from the long rustic pine dining table to the practical modern kitchen

a taupe crocodile-skin-covered low table, or light fixtures made from sheep horn. They are all what the French call *coups de cœur* (love at first sight) often brought back from her frequent travels across the globe.

Perhaps the most "indigenous" piece of furniture in the chalet is a chair made from moose antlers (complemented by a series of antlers hung on the opposite wall) that was "subversively" painted white "to transform a potentially kitsch object into a thing of beauty" says Jocelyne. The artworks, which include several

OPPOSITE: The polished steel, contemporary-style practical kitchen was designed to blend with the mineral and wood elements of the chalet.

ABOVE AND LEFT: Jocelyne Sibuet enjoys cooking traditional bourgeois family-style cuisine—"the kind of dish you throw into a big pot, let it simmer, and then put it on the table"—whenever friends or her children, Marie and Nicolas, come to stay. The pantry, with a whitewashed antique grandfather clock.

ABOVE LEFT AND RIGHT: The downstairs guest bedroom is a warm mix of tangerine-colored walls, a fur bed throw, and a locally salvaged chest of drawers.

OPPOSITE: The sober elegance of the master bedroom is a soothing medley of white furs and wood to create a restful atmosphere. The lamps are by Kevin Reilly.

monochromatic paintings by the Italian painter Monti, and a framed photo of a snowy forest from a gallery in Moscow, all add to this purposeful aura of tranquillity.

Although Jocelyne says that she always strives for uniformity in material and color (which, in this case, is essentially wood from floor to ceiling), the chalet's modernity also emerges through the odd contemporary accessory, such as a transparent glass hanging light fixture or a crystal *objet d'art*. In addition to a few treasured old pieces, such as an eighteenth-century armoire or a carved antique door, the owner also used gilded Baroque pieces—a bedroom lamp mounted on a gold church ornament, for example— to offset the monochromatic pale hues. "I'm very attracted to the Baroque style and it's also part of the heritage of Savoie," explains Jocelyne, referring to the trail of nineteenth-century Baroque chapels scattered across the Alpine valleys. "The Italian influence is also very strong from the days of trading."

Everything in "Hauteluce" has been designed for conviviality, from the long untreated pine table in the dining room to the practical modern kitchen, where the owner enjoys cooking a simmering pot of creamy chestnut soup or a *blanquette de veau* for guests on a cold winter night.

LEFT: The bedroom décor combines a variety of textures and natural elements, such as the crocodile-skin dressing table, adorned with a variety of seashell necklaces.

RIGHT: A daybed for lounging.

RIGHT BELOW AND OPPOSITE: The sleek geometric lines of the modern bathroom in stone and marble create balance with the rustic wood. The owner looked to the natural environment as a guiding force in the decoration of the chalet, using all the local materials at hand.

The full-length windows of the dining room open onto the sunlit garden patio, a slated wood deck that faces the vast wooded slope. In the backyard pasture, a white life-size sculpted cow grazes, blending perfectly with the freshly fallen snow; further on, a tiny burbling mountain stream runs through the garden. In summer months, the terrain is blanketed with white edelweiss and tiny pale pink mountain flowers, with one corner reserved for the thriving vegetable patch.

"Depending on the season, I have different sets of handmade porcelain that I've found during my travels in the south of France or in Italy. In the winter, the dishes are variations of white and taupe. In the warm weather, I set the table with different shades of green and white to blend with the wild beauty of the landscape."

Jocelyne's small study is filled with books and photos, reflecting her strong sense of family. Her daughter, Marie, often stays in the cozy tangerine-walled downstairs bedroom, adjacent to the entrance. "I wanted a bright color and a slightly more contemporary feel," says Jocelyne. "No house should have a 'total look', but I do have a thing about symmetry and pairs—two chairs, two closets—it's a bit theatrical but it works."

"I remember once hearing Hubert de Givenchy talk about his idea of elegance in fashion. He defined it in four words—simplicity, sobriety, precision, and harmony. That always stayed with me and is what I try to create in my own interiors."

OPPOSITE: The rural eighteenth-century-style bastide "Les Confines" was rendered more elegant by lime-washing the facade, realigning and enlarging the windows, and repainting the shutters in a natural shade of green that would be harmonious with the garden. "The five magnificent plane trees and the underground source were a real draw," says owner Dominique Lafourcade, whose passion for gardens is reflected in the artistic design of the bastide's interiors. In place of an unsightly metal shed in front of the house, the owners dug out an oval pond filled with water lilies and connected it to a long central ribbon of water, which serves as the geometric "spinal column" of the landscaped garden.

THIS PAGE: A view from the bastide terrace of Dominique Lafourcade's landmark garden, bordered by trellises covered with vines and wisteria. The 20-acre property includes two swimming pools bordered by greenery, a flower and vegetable garden, a fruit orchard, and a fanciful African garden hemmed in by bamboo with rare exotic plants. The smaller southwest-facing dining terrace faces a garden of clipped ornamental round hedges. "It's the perfect spot to enjoy the last rays of light before sunset," says the owner.

Wedged between Saint Rémy de Provence and Avignon, the sleepy medieval village of Noves is perhaps best known historically for its famed descendant, Laura de Noves, the fourteenth-century muse of Francesco Petrarch, whose beauty was celebrated in his poems. There's a decidedly timeless aura to this uncharted pocket of Provence, and the same could be said of "Les Confines," a stately eighteenth-century-style ocher-yellow bastide, situated just outside of town.

LES CONFINES
NOVES, PROVENCE

Flanked by towering plane trees, the green-shuttered country manor sits across from a vast expanse of elaborate gardens. From the pebbly front terrace, embellished with large glazed Anduze pots filled with lavender, this stunning perspective of luxuriant greenery begins with an ornamental pond of floating water lilies. Between the rows of cypress trees and topiary hedges—all meticulously clipped into geometric arches, squares, and ornamental spheres—is a cutting garden of roses,

peonies, and azaleas, and long wooden trellises covered with mauve and white wisteria.

Indeed, at first glance, the bastide's three-story lime-washed facade seems to have weathered centuries of blazing sunshine, Mistral winds, and winter storms. In fact, Dominique Lafourcade, an artist and self-taught landscaper, and her architect husband, Bruno, acquired the 20-acre property in 1989, and have since invented everything at "Les Confines" from scratch.

"There was nothing here but a flat, fallow wheat field, a few plane trees in front of the dilapidated farmhouse, and an ugly metal shed," Dominique explains. "It had belonged to the Chauvet family, who were well-known landowners in the region, yet they never set foot here. Aside from a few

ABOVE: Dominique Lafourcade designed the picture frames with seashells and other salvaged materials. The lamp is an original creation fabricated with cutouts of painted tin cans.

RIGHT: The cozy winter living room is a fanciful mix of trompe l'œil murals, lamps, and mirror frames by Dominique and faux animal skin chairs. The floral vases by Julie Tareaud and Cliousclat green earthenware plates are part of the owners' vast collection of porcelain.

LEFT: The former stable was converted into a west-facing salon and library, used as a second winter living room. The owners added the gray country-style fireplace adorned with spheres, a subtle reference to the adjacent jardin des boules (garden of the balls).

OPPOSITE: The dining room is a patchwork of color and whimsy, filled with local animal-themed bric à brac and garden flowers. Dominique Lafourcade's trompe l'œil murals depict the couple's favorite landscapes from their travels to the far corners of the globe.

BELOW: The Provençal-style cupboards are filled with pieces from the family collection of eighteenth- and nineteenth-century china, including Dominique Lafourcade's own floral designs of Gien porcelain.

sheep and a peasant farmer who lived here, it was essentially an abandoned property. We called it our 'sleeping beauty... without the beauty!' at first, but recognized its potential right away."

However, the most decisive factor was the presence of an underground natural source, a treasured asset to the sun-baked soil of Provence. The first thing the owners did was erect a small wind-powered pump to get the water flowing through ribbon-like paths throughout the property.

Pooling their multiple professional talents, the husband-and-wife team designed a plan that would preserve the spirit of a farmhouse and salvage as much as possible from the original construction. "We even kept the old shutters and later used them as doors for our garden huts," Dominique says. "It was also important to respect the original volume of each space." Bruno, whose specialty is the renovation and transformation of homes and instilling them with a classic eighteenth-century spirit, was able to create a more "noble" effect by realigning some of the west-facing facade windows. By elevating one layer of red roof tiles, he also reconfigured the attic space by opening up the small dark rooms without changing the

LEFT: The cheery country kitchen is the central hub of activity since the owners are also passionate cooks. The antique wooden farm table, found locally, was given a Verona marble tabletop. For added color, the simple chairs, rescued from a brocante market, were painted blue. In bold contrast, the walls are decorated with Salernes ceramic tiles from Alain Vagh.

RIGHT: A collection of copper pans adorns the walls. The marble mortar, a typical Provençal utensil, is used to make aioli and pistou.

> "We're fanatical about collecting local dishware and pottery," says Dominique. "But it's a luxury to be able to change plates according to your mood."

harmony of the building's exterior. Above all, "Les Confines" reflects the artistry of Dominique, who was born in nearby Avignon and initially studied interior design at the Paris Ecole Camondo. After years of designing Gien porcelain with her vibrantly colored floral and vegetal-inspired patterns, she developed her knowledge of Provençal and Italian-style gardens into a personalized style of landscaping that always includes a touch of whimsy.

"I don't like to feel confined, and, for me, the garden is an extension of the house," says Dominique, whose sunlit loft-style atelier is a joyous pandemonium of work-in-progress and offers a sweeping view of the verdant property from the tall, curved sash windows and French doors.

Since Dominique and Bruno are both fond of cooking, the real hub of activity at "Les Confines" is the spacious country kitchen. Amid an array of copper pots and a wall lined with brightly colored Salernes tiles, simplicity and functionality prevail: straw baskets dangle from the ceiling; others sit on the wooden table, stacked with hand ;ickedked vegetables and herbs. The cupboards—local farmhouse antiques—are

OPPOSITE: Dominique's garden-view atelier, originally two dark rooms, was opened up and reconfigured into an artist's loft with high ceilings and large sash windows to maximize the dazzling light. Amid a jumble of straw baskets and tools for the garden are a multitude of original works-in-progress: lamps, picture frames, hanging mobiles made of salvaged tin cans, models for life-sized children's doll houses, and architectural drawings for garden designs.

all lined with Dominique's Gien china but for everyday use there's also a large collection of Provençal yellow and green Cliousclat earthenware from a small potter's village in the Drôme.

"Changing décor is one of the greatest luxuries," Dominique says, which is why the couple decided to build contrasting dining rooms on each side of the kitchen, along with an additional al fresco dining porch on the southwest side of the bastide, next to the living room.

The small sitting room and living room, formerly the stable, were refurbished with fireplaces and retain a rustic quality, since nearly every lamp, picture frame, painting, drawing, or trompe-l'oeil collage is one of Dominique's handmade creations. "Everything is

made with materials I happen to find—tin cans, seashells, pebbles, bits of wood or bamboo, pods, pine cones, apricot and peach pits—nothing gets thrown away," she says.

The narrow stone stairs, which were left in their original state, lead to the second story of the house, which is divided into five bedrooms. Everything, from the wooden four-poster canopy bed in the master suite to the hand-stitched flowery quilts, was found in local antique markets. Dominique has also kept many of her early creations, including an armoire made of vintage cigar boxes and the children's room headboard adorned with hand-drawn labels of flowers.

The third level comprises two large sloping-walled bedrooms under the eaves and an attic. A dazzling array of trophies abounds in the former room of their son, Alexandre, a racer and noted

LEFT: An upstairs guest bedroom with an armchair from the family's collection. The base of the lamp that sits on the small table was made from a pile of superimposed books. The artist chose all the curtain fabrics and linens.

ABOVE: Each of the eighteenth-century Provençal-style bedrooms is unique, filled with beautifully appointed furnishings and tall French windows.

architect who now heads the Lafourcade firm. Bruno Lafourcade, who is also a car aficionado, says that one of his priorities was to build a garage large enough to house the family collection of vintage Bugattis.

Among the many original constructions at "Les Confines," Dominique constructed a wooden "temple" at the edge of the property which picks up the last rays of the setting sun, and framed the perspective with a circle of hedges and a porthole window inside the house. Another romantic vantage point is the "belvedere," a custom-built wooden circular spiral staircase and platform atop the century-old plane tree.

Hidden away in the garden next to the vegetable patch and the fruit orchard, is the summer house, dubbed "Piccola," a converted stable that the couple uses as a weekend retreat, fully equipped with solar-heated shower and tiny kitchen. "We originally built the cabin for our donkey, Piccolo, but after one year he became odious and we had to give him away," recounts Dominique with a smile. "Our idea was to convert it into a kind of garden version of a Marseillais fisherman's hut, which is why we painted it the same traditional cobalt blue as the little boats."

Though only meters away from their deeply comfortable yellow bastide, this spare mini-cottage equally reflects the spirit of the Lafourcades' distinctive approach: "home" is always a glowing interior space that mirrors the owners' love of nature. As Petrarch wrote, referring to his beloved Laura de Noves, "... from a little village a sun is given, such that the place, and nature, praise themselves, out of which so lovely a lady is born to world." The same might be said of today's lovely lady of Noves, "Les Confines."

ABOVE LEFT: The bathroom for the master bedroom with an antique claw-foot tub.

ABOVE: The guest bedroom with a mix of stripes and flowers. The original painted headboard and seashell mirror frame are by Dominique Lafourcade.

OPPOSITE: The yellow master bedroom with a garden view. The canopy four-poster, fabricated by Brone, was custom designed by the owners, right down to the faux fauve skin trim, a playful reference to Dominique's passion for animals and nature.

Carved into the rock above the Grande Corniche, perched almost a thousand feet above sea level, the old village of Roquebrune is a labyrinth of ancient pink-brick stacked houses, steep winding cobblestone stairways, and vaulted archways. From almost any vantage point, there's a dizzying view of the Cap-Martin peninsula bordering Monaco. Unlike other touristy boutique-glutted medieval villages on the Riviera, Roquebrune's tranquil authenticity has made it one of the most sought-after places to own property.

L'AUMÔNERIE

ROQUEBRUNE

The village is best known for its tenth-century castle and dungeon, reputedly the earliest feudal château in France and sole example of the Carolingian style. Strategically situated to ward off attacks, the Grimaldis (who ruled Roquebrune for five centuries before they sold the village to France in 1861) later remodeled the castle. By the early twentieth century, when Roquebrune Cap-Martin's coastal strip had begun to attract the era's prominent political and artistic figures (including Winston Churchill, WB Yeats, Coco Chanel, Le Corbusier, and Eileen Gray), a wealthy Englishman, Sir William Ingram, arrived on the scene. He decided to purchase the old village château in 1911 and add a mock medieval tower.

Legends still abound in this lovely remote village, beginning with the popular belief that it is miraculously blessed. At the height of the great plague in 1467,

ABOVE: On the way to L'Aumônerie is a tiny village square where local residents sit outside to enjoy the view from the street.

LEFT: The landscaped garden and geometric miniature boxwood hedges combine a colorful mix of purple monkey grass and purple-leaved begonias. A copy of a faun's head was found at a local architectural salvage store to replace the decaying stone fountain.

OPPOSITE: The old village of Roquebrune is a maze of vaulted archways and ancient stone, including the local post office, adorned with late Roman Byzantine ornaments. A view of the Principality of Monaco from L'Aumônerie's loggia. The original Gregorian Gothic windows in the dining room were salvaged and enlarged by dropping them to floor level and adding wrought-iron copies in the same patterns as in the arc of the window. A view of the four-story facade from the garden.

RIGHT: The small, vaulted, yellow-ocher dining room on the ground floor is used year-round for informal meals. Here, as on the upper levels, the flooring was restored with terra-cotta tiles from Salernes. The heavy orange curtains made from sturdy ship canvas are identical to the fabric chosen by former owners, antiquarian Raymond Poteau and Vogue photographer Henry Clarke.

OPPOSITE: The seventeenth-century orange-walled sunlit loggia, where many of the plants and furniture date to the 1950s, is a combination of North African and vintage design. The current owner, John-Mark Horton, has preserved this room—his favorite in the house—exactly as it was when Poteau and Clarke entertained here, from the brick flooring with marble inserts to the orange folding chairs, which belonged to Poteau.

the Roquebrune inhabitants were spared from the clutches of the epidemic after praying nine consecutive days to the Virgin. Even today, every August, locals commemorate their history with an elaborate staging of Christ's Passion and a procession that begins at the Sainte-Marguerite church.

L'Aumônerie (The Alms House), whose discreet entrance is on a sloping narrow alley next to the church, has an unusual legacy all its own. Once attached to Sainte-Marguerite by a narrow eleventh-century hallway, the four-story house and guest annex have been a continual work-in-progress, pieced together over the past half-century, as the succession of owners broke through the city walls and consolidated the disparate small neighboring apartments into one home.

"At the outset, there were monks who lived in the house and cultivated the garden," says current owner John-Mark Horton, a Franco-American interior designer. "Traditionally, it's a place where gifts of food or money were left."

Before taking possession of the house in September 1999, John-Mark recounts that his sentimental attachment to the property began when he was a child and used to play in the luxuriant garden of its former owners, Parisian decorator and antiquaire Raymond Poteau and renowned American fashion photographer

Henry Clarke. "My mother also had a house in the village," he says, "and they were old family friends."

During the 1950s and 60s, Poteau and Clarke held mythical sumptuous dinners behind the ancient stone walls of the small but elaborate garden of their Roquebrune villa. Among the invited glitterati were Audrey Hepburn and Greta Garbo, as well as writer Lesley Blanch-Gary, who had a neighboring apartment up the street.

However, it was Princess Grace of Monaco who wrote a glowing description in The Book of Flowers about her friend Raymond Poteau's "secretive and special" cloister-like garden replete with burbling stone fountains and "splashes of color." In a chapter entitled "Some Gardens That I Love," she writes: "The flowers are unpretentious pink belladonnas, white nicotiana, a ginger plant, white petunia, all surrounded by luscious greenery."

Inside the house, the same meticulous care was given to every detail. As a collector of elegant eighteenth-century Provençal and Italian furniture, Raymond Poteau filled L'Aumônerie with handpicked antiques brought back from his travels, as well as rare objects, such as seventeenth-century scientific instruments and globes.

"Both Raymond Poteau and Henry Clarke had a real passion for ceramic tiles and would travel far and wide to get them," explains John-Mark, who has preserved all the original tiling throughout the house, including Raymond's stunning blue-and-white Delft-tiled bathroom. Another leitmotif is the abundant use of travertine stone or metal spheres, adding up to a total of 24 ornamental balls scattered throughout the house and garden.

By 1985, Henry Clarke had joined Poteau in Roquebrune and lived there full-time. Having moved from New York to Paris after the Second World War and worked for *Vogue* for thirty years, Clarke was best known for his celebrity portraits—everyone from European royals to Twiggy, Coco Chanel, and Sophia Loren—but was also considered a pioneer for his early use of Ektachrome film and fashion shoots in exotic destinations.

"In the late 90s, after Raymond's death, Henry fell ill," recalls John-Mark, "and I realized that there would come a day when I would never see their house again. Henry allowed me to photograph everything I wanted to remember." Little did John-Mark dream that these very photos would later serve to recapture the spirit at the alms house as he once knew it.

When Clarke died in 1996, the photographer left his entire estate to the Institut Pastor, requesting that the Roquebrune villa's furnishings and artwork be auctioned by Christie's in Monaco for cancer research. He also bequeathed his historical collection of photography to Musée Galliera in Paris. A year went by, but the Aumônerie and its sadly neglected garden remained empty. "There had been one serious buyer who made an offer, but he backed out at the last minute, claiming that he was too tall for the medieval door frames and low ceilings," says John-Mark. "I was still haunted by the house and I trusted that I was making the right move."

Formerly an orange-walled loggia,
similar to the room below it,
Horton converted Henry Clarke's
quarters on the fourth floor into
a private, more contemporary-
style living room. In addition to
closing up the room and adding
bay windows, the owner
whitewashed the walls and
furnishings, including an antique
wood cabinet salvaged from the
pantry. The pair of wood keyhole
chairs was found at the Nice flea
market. Horton also hung
samples from his own collection
of sixteenth- and seventeenth-
century Andalusian and Italian
ceramic tiles.

Since he acquired the 450 square-meter property in 1999, John-Mark has made a number of practical changes to the living space, beginning by breaking through the walls of a small adjacent apartment on the second story to put in a new modern kitchen, a spacious pantry, and a wine cellar. The former tiny kitchen, inconveniently situated on the ground floor below the dining room ("the food was always cold!"), was reconfigured into two guest bedrooms and bathrooms. John-Mark also decided to drop the ceiling in Raymond's master bedroom to hide two unsightly beams in the middle of the room and to soundproof the space.

On the third level, there are still many traces of Poteau's eclectic tastes. In the eighteenth-century, country-style living room, one of the most striking features is the series of Italian painted doors depicting mythological scenes. Likewise, the orange-walled, Moroccan-style loggia, with a sweeping vista of the coast, looks much the same as it did in the 1950s. Built into one of the outer pillars of the loggia's arch is a convincingly detailed stone replica of a Hellenistic second-century pillar depicting Alexander the Great.

The floors—originally nineteenth-century terra-cotta *tommettes* in poor condition—were replaced and leveled with new rust-colored tiles from Salernes and Ligurian black slate. John-Mark also opened up windows, particularly in the dining room where he changed the

The 1850s library table and Louis Philippe chairs in the dining room were found in Paris at the St Ouen flea market. To add harmony to the room, the cabinetry was designed to match the original walnut woodwork moldings on the fireplace.

ABOVE: An antique painted glass Dutch ship adds a bright touch to the blue and white Delft bathroom.

LEFT, ABOVE RIGHT, AND BELOW: The Delft-tile bathrooms were designed by former owners, Poteau and Clarke, whose vast collection of ceramic tiles was used to decorate many areas of the house.

OPPOSITE: The toile de Jouy bedspread was chosen for its aptly named fabric "America Greeting Europe" and nautical theme. Above the bed: an eighteenth-century French landscape from the owner's private collection. The carpet, a late nineteenth-century Caucasian runner, is also a family piece.

fenestrations into tall Venetian-style windows that look out on to the garden.

Over the years, the owner has furnished the rooms with a mix of family heirlooms—Turkish carpets, Romanian church relics—in an instinctive reinterpretation of his friends' former home. The dining room, for example, a polished wood 1850s French library table, was found in the Paris St Ouen flea market, along with some small sturdy Louis Phillipe-style chairs. Other finds—a pair of Louis XV ballroom chairs and an early twentieth-century sofa from L'Isle-sur-la-Sorgue—were reupholstered in swirling Italian eighteenth-century-style fabrics to soften the austerity of the room.

On the upper floor, John-Mark modified Henry Clarke's quarters by whitewashing the walls of the front rooms, which he now uses as a library, but has carefully preserved the impressive original eighteenth-century English patterned wallpaper of the bedroom.

The mythical, carefully tended garden, lined with boxwood hedges, pink oleander, and roses, lives on as an integral part of the villa's serene harmony with the exterior. "I've been very lucky," John-Mark says. "This house is family to me and it still has a touch of magic for everyone who visits."

VILLA BAULIEU
PROVENCE

Over two thousand years ago, when the Greeks arrived in Marseille, they had the excellent idea to cultivate vines and plant olive trees throughout the Provençal countryside. Today, the small flower-lined village of Rognes, roughly nine miles northwest of Aix-en-Provence, still produces award-winning wines due to exceptional quality of its grapes. The town is also known for its unusual stone— a curious mix of sand, molluscs, and seashells, discovered as early as the Roman Empire. Likewise, the history of this unspoilt tiny pocket of Provence, on the crossroads of five ancient trade routes, is as rich as its fertile soil.

Built atop the ancient volcano crater of the Trévaresse, Villa Baulieu is situated inside a 300-hectare estate bordered by forests of truffle oaks, almond trees, and lush vineyards. Viewed from the majestic pine-shaded walkway leading to the entrance, this Italianate Provençal manor exudes a timeless quality that conjures visions of noblemen on horseback and elegant country fêtes of centuries gone by.

ABOVE: The facade of the castle with its crenelated tower and the majestic cour d'honneur entrance.

OPPOSITE, TOP LEFT: View of the vineyards, Villa Baulieu, and the Alpilles mountains of the Luberon.

OPPOSITE, TOP RIGHT: Above the entrance to the summer kitchen, formerly the stable.

OPPOSITE, BOTTOM LEFT: The main door of the Villa Baulieu. A coat of arms figures above the door that dates to the Counts of Candolle, depicting a gold and azure shield with two lions, each holding a banner marked "Aide Dieu en bon Chevalier" (Aid God as faithful Knight).

OPPOSITE, BOTTOM RIGHT: One of two stone grottoes on the estate, lined with fossilized seashells.

The sprawling property once belonged to the Counts of Provence, who ruled the fiefdom beginning in 1576, under the reign of Henri III. As the property was passed from one aristocratic family to another, the estate also underwent several modifications during the late seventeenth and early eighteenth centuries. Essentially a country bastide, the Jullien/Julhans family transformed the Baulieu mansion by laying

BELOW LEFT: A Louis XIV armchair (fauteuil d'apparat) from the family collection.

BOTTOM LEFT: A detail from the eighteenth-century Provençal chandelier in the music room.

BELOW: The ornate sculpted white plaster chimneypieces, called gypseries, are typical of sixteenth- and seventeenth-century Provence.

OPPOSITE: The music room, with a harpsichord and a nineteenth-century Steinway, for informal evening concerts among guests. The seventeenth-century portrait above the chimney is one of several examples of a tondo, a Renaissance term for a circular work of art.

OPPOSITE: The 33-foot long Renaissance-style walnut dining room table was custom-designed for the house and can seat up to 24 guests. During the restoration process, the owners rediscovered the original 1635 decorative painted motifs on the wood ceiling beams that were hidden under a layer of plaster.

ABOVE: Another example of a reconstructed Provençal plaster gypserie chimney, built by Pierre Caron and his team of exceptional local craftsmen.

sturdy basalt foundations and rebuilding it in an Italianate villa style, circa 1635. Given that the Aixois countryside is located midway between Rome and Paris, it was not surprising that the Italian influence in architecture flourished in Provence during this period.

The castle's next notable change came in 1805, when four crenelated towers were added to the main house. During the same period, the surrounding 54-acre park (where a romantic seventeenth-century stone temple of love still stands) was transformed by the creation of

a formal French-style garden filled with roses and irises. Similarly, the ornately carved stone statues, fountains, and ponds, fed by an ancient source that runs beneath the property, all contributed to a new air of grandeur.

However, after two centuries of successive owners— among them the Counts of Candolle, family of the renowned botanist, and the Barlet, a Lyonnais silk manufacturing family—the thriving vineyard estate of Baulieu gradually fell into a state of disrepair. In 2001, the Guénant family bought the property and immediately

decided to rescue the 350 acres of vineyards. This entailed replanting many of the vines and becoming actively involved in boosting the quality of the wine production at every level. A decade later, the Château Beaulieu vineyards have become the leading winery for the AOC Coteaux d'Aix appellation, producing almost a million bottles of rosé per year. Bérengère Guénant, the daughter of the current owners, heads the operation of the domain.

While reviving the vineyards, Pierre and his wife Nicole also faced the daunting task of renovating the three-story château, which took seven full years of work. "When we arrived, the house was in a complete state of abandonment—*dans son jus*—in its original condition," says

OPPOSITE: **The sixteenth-century monastery table and brightly painted nineteenth-century English chairs lend a warm touch to the kitchen.**

BELOW: **Some of the family's antique silver pieces are on display in the kitchen.**

RIGHT: **Owner Nicole Guénant's collection of English china and crystal.**

Pierre Guénant. "There hadn't been any veritable work or modernization here since 1782. The plumbing and electricity dated from the early 1900s. There were huge ugly pipes everywhere."

As the estate had been uninhabited for approximately twenty years, the park was also overrun with weeds and brambles. "You couldn't even see the fountains," says Pierre. "We rebuilt the crenelated wall surrounding the main courtyard." Much to the owners' delight, they discovered that two of the three Roman aqueducts on the property were still intact, as well as an altar dedicated to the Goddess of Springs, which dates back to the Augustan Age. Another surprising find were the two small

cave-like grottoes, built in the fifteenth century, which are lined with volcanic fossils. The surrounding forest, planted with chestnut, pine, cypress, walnut, almond, olive, and plane trees, also includes ten acres of truffle oaks. "Truffles are the pride and joy of Rognes," says Bérengère. "Our neighbor's dog hunts them for us every year."

With the help of architect Guy-Marie Kieffer and a team of artisans, the castle was reconfigured into a twelve-bedroom home that includes a library, a music room, a smoking room, a country-style kitchen, a refurbished glassed-in

ABOVE LEFT: A nineteenth-century Murano glass chandelier, bought by the Guénant family during their frequent trips to Venice.

TOP RIGHT: Detail from the Tuscan marble chimney.

ABOVE CENTER AND RIGHT: Details of the gilded early eighteenth-century décor of the Italianate bedroom.

OPPOSITE: The bedroom pays homage to the castle's former resident, Guillaume de Julien, who gave the estate its present appearance. The prevailing Italian influence ranges from furnishings such as the ornate Sicilian throne armchair to the terrazzo marble flooring, invented in Venice.

OPPOSITE: Another bedroom was created in place of a sitting room, with a Louis XVI-style canopy bed. The rare eighteenth-century "deux pigeons" wallpaper was originally in the ground-floor drawing room of the castle.

ABOVE LEFT: The mirror, canopy bed, and decorative ornaments are all original furnishings found in the Baulieu attic.

ABOVE RIGHT: The drop-leaf crystal chandelier hangs from a painted ceiling, possibly done by one of the castle's former owners, Pierre Robineau de Beaulieu, who arrived in 1754 and was a well-known artist of his era. Some of Robineau's works are on display at the Musée Granet in Aix-en-Provence.

orangery, and a number of small sitting rooms and parlors. The décor was largely inspired by the style typical of the Louis XVI period and a touch of eighteenth-century Italian splendor.

Among the many steps involved in the long process of bringing the walls back to life, the Guénant family found old painted beams from the seventeenth century, situated both on the ground floor and the antechamber of the first floor. "Of course, we felt obliged to restore them," says Pierre, an art connoisseur who is also a distinguished member of the Commission of Acquisitions at the Louvre.

The sumptuous antique furnishings and museum-quality artwork were carefully selected from a variety of sources. "We knew what we wanted, but it has taken almost ten years," says Pierre Guénant. Essentially, he recounts, about one-tenth of the furnishings was retrieved from the attic of the Villa Baulieu, such as the impressively restored gilded Louis XVI canopy bed, one of many neglected treasures that was salvaged. The rest of the furniture were brought in from the family's collection or purchased while traveling throughout Europe. These unique pieces—an elegant

One key feature in the restoration of the château was maintaining the Italian and Provençal influence of its former owners. The furnishings were all selected to illustrate the stratification of the estate's rich history

Baroque eighteenth-century chest of drawers by Johann August Nahl, or a stunning Murano glass chandelier—are as eye-catching as they are harmonious with the décor.

Some of the other decorative decisions involved sprucing up some of the original fittings. One example is the unusual patterned wallpaper, formerly in the large drawing room on the ground floor, which was stripped, cleaned, and reapplied to the walls of one of the spacious bedrooms upstairs. "The wallpaper has even got a name, *deux pigeons* (two pigeons), and is classified at the Musée de Papier Peint in Rixheim, Alsace." Apparently, says Pierre, the Villa Baulieu is the only house in France where it is still in place.

One of the most striking features of the dining room and living room are the gypseries—elaborate molded and sculpted white plaster chimneypieces, typical of sixteenth-century and early seventeenth-century Provence. "We decided to replace the existing eighteenth-century fireplaces with something more exceptional, and asked craftsman Pierre Caron and his team to re-create the exact style. They are true artists," says the owner.

"Whenever we have guests," says Pierre with a smile, "I tell them straightaway: please, I don't want you to feel at home—I want you to feel in my home."

OPPOSITE: The owners transformed a small alcove in a bathroom with all the modern amenities, a claw foot tub, and a view of the park.

ABOVE: A 1900s-style guest bathroom, equipped with a circular shower attachment that used to be worn around the neck while bathing to protect a lady's hair from getting wet.

MAISONS BOHÈMES

In the French tradition of free-spirited affection for the unconventional, the bohemian interior is an artful mix of antique, vintage, and handcrafted treasures, rescued from auctions and flea markets, or retrieved from family attics. Serendipity prevails, but that does not exclude careful attention to deep comfort and refinement. Whether a guest-room gypsy caravan ablaze with color or a Venetian-inspired bathroom resembling a theater, the element of surprise is inherent to this medley of styles. Characterized by touches of idiosyncratic or whimsical design, these nineteenth- or early twentieth-century homes have become mirrors of the current owners, who make full use of the artist's studio or writer's study within their living space for their own creativity.

OPPOSITE: An authentic restored Romanian gypsy caravan, used as a guest room, sits in the garden under the century-old eucalyptus tree. The dining terrace under a trellis of wisteria. The table is a composite of salvaged wood from Senegalese fishing boats. View of the facade and the stone lap pool, built by the owners.

RIGHT: The fabrics and decor inside the caravan are from a variety of countries, from India to Morocco and Spain, and more locally, from Provence.

When artist Paul Signac arrived in St Tropez by boat in 1892, he wrote to his mother that he had rented a little wooden beach shack "lost in the pines and roses," near the Canoubiers Bay, a short distance from the village. "I have enough here to work for a lifetime—I've just discovered happiness!" he enthused to Henri Matisse, who joined Signac and a little colony of artists to explore the pure colors and dazzling light of the Midi.

LOU MAZET DE L'ESTAGNET
ST TROPEZ

Thirty years after Matisse painted his 1904 masterwork "Luxe, Calme et Volupté" on the tranquil shores of this unspoiled sleepy fishing village, St. Tropez had begun to attract a literary crowd, beginning with French author Colette, who bought a modest villa, La Treille Muscate, in the 1930s, situated outside of town on the Route des Salins. She swam twice a day, plucked fruit from her garden, drank wine from the local vineyards, and danced at the festive *bals* in the lantern-strung square, informing her bewildered Parisian friends that she'd found total rejuvenation in life's simple pleasures. Once the word was out, other writers, directors, and actors followed suit. But even throughout Brigitte Bardot's 1950s glamorous heyday, when film crews descended on the town, the bohemian authentic village spirit of St Tropez still survived amid the glitz and glitter.

This relaxed seaside atmosphere was precisely what French author, playwright, and filmmaker Marcel Pagnol was seeking when, in 1963, he and his wife bought a *mazet* (a little mas) across from the Canoubiers beach, on the same

LEFT: An eclectic jumble of antique furnishings from brocante markets all over Europe, collected over the years by the owners, Viviane and Bruno Vidal de la Blache.

ABOVE: The living room is a showcase for the extensive collection of globes, a tribute to Bruno's great-great-grandfather, Paul Vidal de la Blache, the famous founder of modern geography.

OPPOSITE: Among the vintage furnishings are two leather Charles Eames chairs, found at attic sale markets. The stone fireplace was built by Marcel Pagnol during the 1960s.

road as Colette's property. An austere, thick-walled house with only four rooms, surrounded by vines and a jungle of bamboo, Pagnol purchased it on first sight from a widow whose husband had worked in the nearby torpedo factory.

Celebrated for his Provence-based novels, *Jean de Florette*, *Manon des Sources*, and film classic *The Baker's Wife*, the 68-year-old writer spent the next ten summers at this peaceful refuge where he could write undisturbed, unlike at his inland home in the Var. There was a breezy tiled patio shaded by an ancient plane tree, and another large terrace upstairs with a partial view of the burnished blue sea. More unusual were the three wells on the property, which date back to 1890 and have remained intact to this

day. "It wasn't comfortable, but absolutely charming," wrote his wife, Jacqueline, when describing their rustic new quarters. The shower and bathroom were outside in the garden, but Pagnol, who apparently loved to tinker, added a small kitchen for barbecues behind the house. The Canoubiers beach, only steps away, was filled with shacks selling grilled shrimp and mussels for improvised picnics.

Wearing what he called his "mason's uniform"—old trousers, a sweater, and espadrilles—Pagnol would shop in the village fish and produce market, then collect his *fougasse* (a Provençal bread made with olive oil, olives, and bacon) from the baker's shop, stop for newspapers and notebooks, and then spend the rest of the day at work.

Marcel Pagnol stayed at his beloved "L'Estagnet" ("my cloister... sheltered from the world's dangers") until his death in 1974, whereupon Jacqueline sold the house to the Le Sidaner family. The new owners, who were descendants of the well-known late nineteenth-century intimist painter Henri Le Sidaner, had homes elsewhere and seldom set foot on the property. As time passed, the villa fell into a complete state of disrepair.

In 1988, when Viviane Vidal de la Blache, a fashion designer and boutique owner, and her husband Bruno pushed open the gate to view the overgrown garden and dilapidated house for sale, they were not discouraged. "The prices were totally inaccessible everywhere else in St Tropez," says Viviane. "In a matter of moments, we knew what we could do to re-create the charm it once

OPPOSITE: The kitchen is a colorful assembly of retrieved and repainted furnishings from flea markets. The owner kept the original Provençal floor tiles, which date back to its construction.

ABOVE LEFT: A wooden buffet that was made in the US, then brought to St Tropez.

ABOVE: The front room, once an outdoor terrace where the original wells still stand, is often used as a dining room.

RIGHT: The bold-hued collection of vintage ceramics range from local vintage pitchers to an African soup tureen.

With their sense of original style, Viviane and Bruno Vidal de la Blache transformed the rudimentary "L'Estagnet" into a free-spirited colorful fête

Pagnol's terrace study was reconfigured into a red-walled,
loft-like space for lounging and an adjoining master bedroom

ABOVE AND ABOVE RIGHT: A
marble-topped bistro table. The wall
light fixture was made from a salvaged
locomotive headlight. A 1930s walnut
armoire, also found in a local market.

OPPOSITE: The Armenian four-
poster bed was once owned by singer
Charles Aznavour. The wicker chairs
are decorated with cushions hand-
embroidered by Viviane's grandmother.

had. But in the beginning, there wasn't even any heating. There we
were, a family with three young children—we went to sleep bundled
up in sweaters and socks."

Born in Paris, Viviane entered the world of prêt-à-porter at
the age of eighteen, working alongside her father, Zyga Pianko,
creator of the Pierre d'Alby label, who also launched budding
designers including Agnes B. and Daniel Hechter. Viviane's late
husband, Bruno (whose great-great-grandfather was the illustrious
founder of modern geography, Paul Vidal de la Blache), had also
traveled the world and become a dealer in *brocantes* (second-hand
attic treasures) and antiques.

With their shared sense of original style, the couple transformed
Pagnol's rudimentary "L'Estagnet" into a free-spirited colorful fête:
a medley of objets d'art, paintings, trinkets, African masks, gauzy

"You live sheltered from the world's dangers... It's my cloister," wrote Pagnol

fabrics hung from the ceiling like mosquito netting, North African carpets, artfully draped silk scarves from Viviane's local fashion boutique, Bla-Bla, family heirlooms, hand-embroidered pillows, antique toys, and a jumble of furnishings from auctions or local markets.

One of the first reconfigurations was enclosing Pagnol's second-story covered terrace, formerly used as a study, and transforming it into a warm orange-red walled loft-like space. "We kept the open wooden beams and old lamps, had walls built, and put in large bay windows," Viviane explains. The en-suite bathroom—a tub partially concealed by a huge Picasso banner—is adjacent to a spacious sitting room. Some of Viviane's favorite finds include a vintage desk that was once a sorting cabinet from the St Tropez post office, as well as her unusual collections of beds. "I sleep on French singer Charles Aznavour's Armenian-style four-poster," she says with a smile. "He

OPPOSITE: One corner of Pagnol's former study on the first floor was transformed into a guest room, dubbed "la chambre des femmes," decked out with gauzy Indian fabrics. In the corner, a vintage piece used to store maps.

ABOVE LEFT: The bed in the guest room features an original painted headboard by the contemporary Niçois artist, Ben.

ABOVE RIGHT: One of several paintings of women in various poses that adorn the upstairs guest room.

LEFT: The loft space includes an en-suite bathroom with a floor-to-ceiling banner of Picasso. The ethnic-style shawls, scarves, hats, and bags are all sold in Viviane Vidal de la Blache's exclusive boutique, Bla-Bla, in St Tropez.

OPPOSITE: The desk originally came from the St Tropez post office, used for sorting mail. The chair, salvaged from a church, dates from the nineteenth century.

pioneer Paul Vidal de la Blache. Some hang from the ceiling, others sit on the long wooden table and give off a luminous glow at night. Serendipity and comfort, says Viviane, have always been key factors in her decorative style. A giant roulette wheel from a casino in Cannes sits on a table in the center of the room; the huge wooden floor-to-ceiling bookcase is actually a carpenter's work tool cabinet, purposely left in its weathered condition.

The kitchen was extended for practicality's sake, diminishing the size of the front garden terrace, but anything that was salvageable was preserved, including the original red and white lozenge tiles. The country-style cupboards are lined with an assortment of brightly glazed 1950s-style crockery, often found in flea markets.

"I met Pagnol's gardener once," recounts Viviane. "He said that the well—which used to be on the garden terrace, but is now part of my kitchen—provided water for the schoolchildren at the Sainte-Anne school nearby."

The garden, decked out with paper lanterns strung from trees and a giant teak Indonesian daybed by the stone pool, invites relaxation. Over in a corner, parked under a eucalyptus tree, is another recently acquired "irresistible" gem: a fully refurbished green gypsy caravan that serves as an extra guest bedroom.

It is also one more reminder of the bohemian St Tropez of yesteryear. Far from the yacht-clogged harbor and jet-setters' playground, "L'Estragnet" has remained true to the artistic spirit of a secret hideaway where one of France's most famed twentieth-century writers was able to enjoy Mediterranean life to its fullest.

owned a house in St Tropez. When he left, all of his belongings were for sale. The bed originally came with a very ornate headboard, but Bruno eventually sold it." A more recent acquisition, in the guest bedroom, is a crimson headboard painted by the contemporary Niçois artist Ben, renowned for his humorous childishly scrawled proverbs (here, *dormir autrement*—sleep in a different way).

The downstairs living room needed little modification since Pagnol had built a brick fireplace that is still functional. One of the most striking features of the room is the collection of globes of every dimension and decade, an obvious tribute to the geographic

Behind a weathered wooden gate, at the end of a tranquil leafy lane, the family home of the Count and Countess de Rohan Chabot is strikingly different from most Parisian dwellings, beginning with its unique location at the edge of the 16th arrondissement.

AN ARTIST'S ATELIER
PARIS

Tucked away inside the Villa Montmorency, a gated community reputed for its wealthy high-profile residents, this relatively modest house is a cross between a bohemian artist's garden studio and a sophisticated miniature *hôtel particulier* filled with period furnishings and family portraits.

Built in 1853, the landmark Villa Montmorency was originally conceived as a peaceful private refuge near the Bois de Boulogne, where many famed actors and writers, including Sarah Bernhardt and André Gide, once sought inspiration. In recent years, this prestigious, lush property has now become the home of France's most prominent industrialists and showbusiness stars. Former President Nicolas Sarkozy and Carla Bruni, who live on the street just behind the Villa Montmorency, are also neighbors.

In contrast to the surrounding stately mansions, the fanciful elegance of the de Rohan Chabot's house is obvious from the exterior, adorned with fluttering

OPPOSITE: The living room is an eclectic mix of antique furnishings. The velvet footstools and armchairs were all found at Paris' famed auction, Drouot, the owners' favorite haunt. The patterned carpet is by Madeleine Castaing, and the landscapes by nineteenth-century Dutch artists are auction finds.

ABOVE LEFT: One of the most striking features of the ground-floor sitting room and living room is the eighteenth-century floral patterned wallpaper, manufactured by the Parisian company Prelle.

ABOVE CENTER: A tall bronze candleholder by Joy de Rohan Chabot stands on the landing that leads to the artist's garden studio below.

ABOVE: The artist's atelier and family home, adorned with butterflies painted on the facade.

ABOVE: An eighteenth-century chest with mother-of-pearl and wood inlay.

RIGHT: Joy is particularly fond of nineteenth-century ceramics and has an extensive collection of faience barbotines and vases. A number of family ancestral portraits hang on the walls of the sitting room and living room. The oil painting above the chimney is a portrait of Joy de Rohan Chabot by Catalan artist Joaquim Torrents Llado. Joy has also posed for many famed photographers including Henry Clarke, David Bailey, and Helmut Newton.

brilliant-hued butterflies that were painted onto the upper portion of the white facade. Just above, discreetly perched atop the roof, a terra-cotta rat gargoyle watches over the garden.

"When we arrived in 1973, we bought the property from an unknown painter. At that time, very few celebrities lived here," says Joy de Rohan Chabot, artist and the *maîtresse de maison*. The owners, who divide their time between Paris and their 23-acre family estate—the fifteenth-century fortified castle of Jozerand in Auvergne— wanted a city home that would feel like a cosy *pied-à terre*.

Formerly a simple one-story structure with an attic and a courtyard, the house was gradually transformed and extended to fit the family's needs. "It's like an old shoe that became larger and more comfortable as the years go by," Joy adds with a smile.

Among Joy de Rohan Chabot's many talents are her impressive handyman and masonry skills. Once the family moved in, she recounts that she rolled up her sleeves and set to work installing the electricity and plumbing, and mixing cement to repair the walls. "It was a total disaster, but I made it livable," she says.

Initially, the exposed beams in the attic were so low that they "went straight through the middle of every room," says Joy, who raised the ceiling to create bedrooms for the couple's two sons. "As they got taller, we had to keep raising it even more," she adds.

ABOVE LEFT: Joy de Rohan Chabot's glass-roofed garden atelier, where trees still grow, was formerly a courtyard. It is a showcase for the artist's works-in-progress: cast bronze glass-topped tables and aluminum sculpted mirrors to hand-painted decorative screens and glassware.

ABOVE RIGHT: The ground-floor entrance. The hammered iron banister was designed by the artist.

OPPOSITE: The owners extended the kitchen into a theatrical turn-of-the-century-style orangery for dining. The hanging metallic light fixture was designed by Jansen. All the hand-painted glassware on the table and the fanciful green "Chimères" candleholders were made by the artist. On display on the back wall is a portrait of May Balfour, Joy's grandmother, found by chance at an auction.

Another more recent transformation entailed enlarging the window of the south-facing master bedroom and leveling the rooftop. The converted space is now a flat sun-drenched terrace lined with climbing roses and exotic plants, "so that you feel like you're in the country."

Joy and her husband, Jean de Rohan Chabot, also decided to do away with a formal dining room and use the room as a study. "Maybe it's in reaction to my childhood memory of interminable dinners," says Joy, who was raised in her family's colossal Château de Bussset in Auvergne. "When we entertain guests here, we tend to dine either in the garden, weather permitting, or in one of the sitting rooms."

Ultimately, the most dramatic change was adjusting the size of the tiny kitchen by extending it into what was

Delightful surprises abound, beginning with the eye-catching walls, covered with a bold mix of contrasting eighteenth-century silk floral patterns

formerly an inner courtyard. This required building a room with a sloping wood and glass skylight, in the style of a turn-of-the-century style orangery, replete with mock antique columns and a swirling green wrought-iron décor. Joy de Rohan's own works are on display in a cupboard filled with painted glass dishware. Along with a vast collection of antique Chinese porcelain, the artist is particularly fond of her assortment of late nineteenth-century faience *barbotines*—vases and platters of borderline kitsch renditions of brightly colored marine life, snakes, and animals.

The kitchen dining area is dominated by a large oil portrait of a stylish woman in a black dress with green jade bracelets. "That was my grandmother, May Balfour, done by a well-known painter," says Joy, who says that the artistic influence of the maternal side of her Scottish Balfour ancestry had a considerable impact on her as a child. "One day, my husband Jean was in an art auction and he happened to spot the painting. Someone else wanted to buy it, but he wouldn't hear of it and had to outbid him."

ABOVE: A view of the bathroom and rustic walnut "toilet chair," retrieved from the owners' country home.

OPPOSITE: The downstairs bathroom is filled with antique mirrors collected over the years, including pieces from the Napoleon III era.

Trained at the Ecole des Arts Décoratifs in Paris, Joy de Rohan Chabot's early predilection for drawing steadily developed into design. Today, the artist's glass-roofed studio, situated on the garden level where a giant begonia, ficus, and eucalyptus tree still grow, is a veritable showcase of work-in-progress: painted decorative screens, glass, metal, and cast bronze chairs, tables, lamps, and mirrors, adorned with a menagerie of birds, butterflies, owls, and other creatures as well as branches, flowers, and vines. Christian Dior now sell her delicate hand-painted glass dishes and goblets, trimmed with dabs of minuscule blossoms.

The first floor is divided into a series of small adjoining rooms beginning with a *petit salon* at the entrance hall with a floral patterned carpet by Madeleine Castaing, followed by two larger sitting rooms and an en-suite winter bedroom. Delightful surprises abound, but the most eye-catching particularity of these rooms is the walls themselves, covered with a bold mix of contrasting eighteenth-century silk floral patterns, manufactured by Prelle. Another of Joy's favorite haunts is Paris' Marché Saint Pierre, a treasure trove for the original fabrics used for all the curtains.

"There are two worlds here—we put the family antiques and ancestral portraits side by side with more contemporary artwork," says Joy. However, many of the furnishings are a harmonious combination of period pieces, all found at antique auctions at Drouot—such as a set of green Napoleon III footstools, or an imposing nineteenth-century mirror—mixed with Joy's luminous bronze and glass butterfly tables and chairs.

Scattered throughout every room are also a multitude of black-and-white family photos, documenting elaborate fêtes, fancy-dress balls, and portraits of Joy, who modeled for Paris *Vogue* in the 1960s, posing for the most famous photographers of the era including Henry Clarke, David Bailey, and Helmut Newton. Upstairs in the bedrooms are Joy's large oil portraits of beloved departed canines and felines, who were also part of the family.

"I love gardens, nature, and animals," the artist says, who is unconcerned that her cats constantly claw some of her best needlepoint chairs to pieces. "What's important to us is waking up in a city like Paris and hearing the birds sing. That's what I call true luxury."

OPPOSITE: The Print Room, which serves as a formal dining room. The antique prints, chosen by the owners, are loosely themed around food and wine, or views of Paris from eras gone by, such as Place des Vosges and Parc Monceau. Nicola Wingate-Saul did the hand-cut trimmings and room design.

RIGHT: Under the curved staircase is a trompe-l'œil library with wallpaper from Paris' Zuber manufacturers.

FAR RIGHT: The Print Room gives onto a small outside courtyard.

BELOW RIGHT: A view of the front entrance from the garden.

To conjure the spirit of Paris' sprawling 17th arrondissement, on the right bank in the northwest edge of the city, one would have begin in the 1860s, when the neighborhood began to take on an artistic vibrancy.

MAISON DU BONHEUR
PARIS

In those years, a group of now-legendary painters and writers, dubbed the "Batignolles Group"—Edouard Manet, Emile Zola, Edgar Degas, Claude Monet, Pierre-August Renoir, and Alfred Sisley, among others—met in the evenings at the Café Guerbois on the Avenue de Clichy, where lively discussions on art forged the aesthetics of impressionism.

The Duke of Orléans had originally purchased the district's lush Parc Monceau, once an enormous vacant field, in the late eighteenth century. Contrary to the formal style of the era, landscape architect Louis Carrogis Carmontelle was commissioned to design an English-style garden with curved paths, Corinthian pillars, statues, and several small-scale architectural follies, such as an Egyptian pyramid, a Chinese fort, and a Dutch windmill. When the spectacular park was sold to the city of Paris in 1861, Napoleon III opened its gates as a public garden. It's no wonder that Claude Monet painted five famous works of the sumptuous vegetation and sun-dappled walkways, which still attract visitors today.

Among notable artistic residents of the 17th arrondissement in the late nineteenth century were composers Maurice Ravel and Gabriel Fauré and actress Sarah Bernhardt, who built herself an immense townhouse, or *hôtel particulier*, on the *très chic* rue Fortuny in 1876.

In contrast to the rows of stylish townhouses reserved for the mistresses of the wealthy bourgeoisie, a thriving industrial working class neighborhood also characterized the 17th arrondissement. It was here, on rue Chazelles, that Alsatian-born sculptor Frédéric-Auguste Bartholdi set up his atelier for the construction of his famed Statue of Liberty in 1881.

With the help of Gustave Eiffel, who constructed the giant goddess' iron skeleton, Bartholdi spent the next three years hammering and forging copper for the 200-ton statue that would measure 150 feet high. Everyone, from luminaries such as Victor Hugo to curious local passers-by, visited the sculptor's numerous workshops, marveling at the sight of a colossal arm or the giant torch in the making.

Hidden away behind a discreet door in this historic neighborhood is La Maison du Bonheur, a three-story white house and garden that also dates back to the late nineteenth century. It seems fitting that current owners, Juliette—a Franco-American who was formerly in interior design and now works in philanthropy—and Jean—an attorney-turned-photographer and artist—have created their off-beat and sumptuously elegant home close to where the symbol of freedom and French and American friendship was born.

"When we bought the house in 1996," says Juliette, "it had been abandoned for quite a while, and it took us two entire years to renovate."

"Rumor has it that the house was a well-known brothel from the 1950s to the 1980s," Jean adds, who has noticed that old-timer taxi drivers still raise their eyebrows when he announces the address.

RIGHT: The winter living room/music room is a colorful mix of Venetian lamps, Biedermeier fruit wood tables, and contemporary art. The footstools were designed by artist and bronze sculptor Franck Evennou, and upholstered with fabrics from Gaggio, a boutique in Venice.

LEFT: The china and hand-painted crystal was especially designed for Juliette and Jean's wedding, themed around a tree motif that symbolizes union and harmony.

BELOW: A view of the kitchen, designed in symmetrical harmony with the yellow walls of the Print Room.

OPPOSITE: The eighteenth-century velvet cloth wall hanging, ornamented with Neo-Classical urns and garlands, was bought at a Christie's auction. The nineteenth-century chandelier is from Sweden. On display: a painting by Timsit.

Each room of the house is a custom-designed creation dreamed up by Juliette and Jean, who worked closely with a team of architects and specialists in interior design to help them carry out their vision. Though the facade remains unchanged, one of the first steps was to do away with the three towering chestnut trees that created unnecessary shade and dominated the garden. These days, the tranquil outdoor patio, where the owners and their children often dine in the summer months, is a joyous mix of wisteria, roses, bamboo, and other exotic plants, shaded by cypresses and a fig tree. It is hard to imagine that the bustling streets of Paris are only steps away.

One of the most radical changes to the house was adding a glass-roofed conservatory, in the style of a *fin-de-siècle* luminous winter garden, at the entrance to the house. Viewed from the exterior, this impressive white wrought-iron frame, built by the English Vale Conservatory Company, is a perfect match with the rest of the house. "It looks like it has been there forever," Juliette says. "Even the light fixture is a replica of a piece designed for a Belgian royal palace." The conservatory is a showcase for artwork, including a number of works combining photographic and painting techniques by American artist Norma Brown Hill and French artist Timsit.

The veritable originality of the home lies in its almost theatrical variation of themes that are also entwined with the owners' longstanding passion for Venice and Anglo-Saxon decorative practices.

The plush winter living room behind the conservatory is used for formal entertaining and as a music room. "We used a lot of Venetian fabrics and velvets from the boutique Gaggio for the curtains and upholstery," says Juliette. "The lamps are also Venetian re-editions, inspired by the works of Mariano Fortuny." In one corner of the room stands a small fruitwood Biedermeier table, one of many pieces that are scattered throughout the house. Among the room's most eye-catching features is an impressive collection of nineteenth-century Venetian glass, combined with a few modern pieces by Boris Sipek and Dale Chihuly.

But perhaps the most visually compelling room is what the owners call their "Print Room," an entrance hall by day, which doubles as a formal dining room in the evening. "The print room was a decorative theme specific to the eighteenth-century Revival Period in England," Juliette recounts. "It was a forgotten art, using old prints glued and varnished onto the walls." Part of the charm, she explains, lies in the decorative ornaments, such as chains, knobs, or borders, which are delicately hand-cut with scissors, then balanced with the prints.

The owners had already begun to collect antique prints of Paris that were especially meaningful to them, including seventeenth-century views of nearby Parc Monceau, when it was a vast field. As it happened, British designer Nicola Wingate-Saul, who has recently brought print rooms back into vogue, was offering a workshop on the technique in London. "I came home from the workshop with all kinds of ideas, but after two days I realized I needed some help,"

says Juliette with a smile. In the end, Wingate-Saul was hired to help the owners complete the painstaking task of putting everything into place.

Although the country-style kitchen is French in spirit, much of the Provincial farmhouse furniture was brought back from the British company Chalon, in London, which includes a freestanding tall wood cupboard that hides the refrigerator and freezer. "The table is by Alain Ducasse, who has since stopped making furniture," says Juliette. Playful touches abound: the hanging light fixtures are an assemblage of glass Campari bottles, designed by Ing Maurer, and the colorful porcelain pieces are hand painted by British ceramic artis, Mary Rose Young.

Upstairs in the master bedroom, the Venetian leitmotif is ever-present, with the same sumptuous fabrics, rare glass pieces, and Biedermeier furnishings as in the living room. The bed features a hand-painted velvet headboard by Russian artist Georges Krivoshey.

OPPOSITE LEFT: Next to the kitchen, the owners designed a cozy sitting room that doubles as a high-tech TV room with a giant screen, completely hidden from view.

OPPOSITE RIGHT: The French Provincial country-style kitchen. The handcrafted brightly colored dishware is by British ceramicist, Mary Rose Young.

ABOVE AND ABOVE RIGHT: A view of the conservatory, a sunlit showcase for contemporary artwork. "The hanging light fixture is a replica of a piece designed for a Belgian princess," says Juliette.

RIGHT: Jean's atelier, filled with brushes, paints, and works in progress.

Stepping into the immense glass-roofed bathroom, the surprising theatrical effect is immediate, which is exactly what the owners had in mind when they designed it. "We found some old décor from an opera performed in Barcelona at an antique store on the Left Bank. It was all rolled up and dusty and we had it mounted and glued on the walls, with the help of Argentine décor painter Roberto Bergero, who painted the walls to match," says Juliette. Dramatically set back in an alcove, the gold-tapped bathtub is draped by heavy curtains, made with antique fabrics from the Bernheim collection, picked up at a Christie's auction. Below the gilded eighteenth-century mirror,

ABOVE: A corner of the Venetian-inspired master bedroom, furnished with Biedermeier pieces from the owners' collection. The curtains are from Chelsea Textiles in the UK.

ABOVE RIGHT: The dramatic glass-roofed bathroom was custom-designed as a theater, with an alcove bathtub surrounded by drapes and a pair of walk-in dressing rooms on either side. A scene from the Venice Carnival in a mask frame hangs on the wall.

BELOW RIGHT: One of the most unique pieces in the home is this combination

marble-topped sink/dresser, decorated with hand-cut vintage print ornaments and varnished. The gold-plated bathroom fittings are by US designer, Shirl Wagner. The nineteenth-century Murano mirror was a Paris flea market find.

OPPOSITE: The master bedroom is a combination of international influences that include an embroidered silk bedspread brought back from India and a canopy bed from London with a velvet headboard hand painted by Russian artist, Georges Krivoshey. Argentine designer Roberto Bergero did the painted ornamental trimmings on the walls.

found at the Paris St Ouen flea market, is one of Juliette's own highly original custom-made creations—the designer bathroom sink was inserted into an Arte Povera-style marble-topped dresser.

"We have taken enormous pleasure in designing this house," says Jean. "The proof is that we haven't changed a thing since we did the work. We named our house La Maison du Bonheur for a good reason."

OPPOSITE: A corner of the studio. The gold mercury mirror is a family piece that dates back to the Regency era. The owners bought the white Louis XV armchair and many of the other furnishings in antique shops in Paris. The eclectic array of antique objets d'art includes an eighteenth-century copy of a bust of an ancient Roman statue.

ABOVE LEFT: "My grandfather was fascinated with history and kept bound editions of all sorts of magazines and periodicals," says Emmanuel.

ABOVE CENTER: Family silver pieces in the living room: a bombonnière for candy, a coffeepot, and a teapot.

ABOVE RIGHT: Breakfast on the deck with a view of the Sacré-Cœur.

Montmartre, the epicenter of bohemian life in *fin-de-siècle* Paris, is renowned for its steep cobblestone streets and the clamorous Place du Tertre, where artists Pierre-Auguste Renoir, Suzanne Valadon, Maurice Utrillo, and Raoul Dufy all had studios.

MONTMARTRE ARTIST'S LOFT
PARIS

Formerly an open slope with windmills, where cows, goats, and chickens wandered freely, the area of Montmartre became notorious in the early twentieth century for its uproarious nightlife and free-flowing inexpensive alcohol, served at the bargemen cafés. Soon the world's most distinguished men of letters and artists were frequenting its legendary cabarets—Le Moulin Rouge, Le Lapin Agile, and Le Chat Noir, where French composer Erik Satie played piano. By the time impoverished painters Pablo Picasso and Amedeo Modigliani and French poets Guillaume Apollinaire and Max Jacob had set up headquarters at the commune Le Bateau-Lavoir in 1904, Montmartre had acquired its reputation as the hotbed for the burgeoning artistic avant-garde.

ABOVE: Above the Louis XVI-era chest hangs a prized artwork: a rare 1640 oil still life painted on wood by Pieter Claesz, interpreted by Emmanuel as a symbolic "meditation on eternity."

RIGHT: A privileged vantage point of the Butte Montmartre, the highest point in Paris. "Candlelit dinners with a backdrop of the illuminated Sacré-Cœur are magical," says Emmanuel. The1940s golden candle sconces that hang on the wall are finds from the Paris flea market.

Inextricably linked to the Montmartre landscape is the imposing Sacré Coeur Basilica, nicknamed the "Alabaster Wedding Cake" church for its white-domed Neo-Byzantine and Romanesque architecture. The 430-foot high church, whose construction began in 1875 and was completed in 1914, sits atop the highest hill in Paris. Now, over a century later, the area is still a magnet for tourists, yet only steps away, there are quiet residential streets on the southern outskirts of Montmartre that form a veritable little neighborhood lined with outdoor markets and leafy squares.

When Emmanuel, an internationally renowned French orchestra conductor, first set foot inside the top-floor studio that is now his

THIS PAGE: The dining corner of the loft, with a Cuban walnut Directoire dining table that extends to seat up to twenty guests. On display in the alcove is a Gandhâra sculpture, circa sixth century, from Pakistan.

OPPOSITE ABOVE: The owners designed the mezzanine study as a separate workspace. The ladder leads to the roof deck, ideal for breakfast or cocktails.

OPPOSITE BELOW: The high ceilings of the former artist's studio and the top-floor location were ideal for the split-level restoration.

home, he was so taken with the mesmerizing view of the Sacré Cœur that any structural disadvantages of the atelier seemed minimal in comparison. "When I was ushered inside by the real estate agent, he took one look at me—I'm six foot four—and told me that this place was not for me," says Emmanuel. "Upstairs, there was a low-ceilinged mezzanine, and downstairs, a tiny kitchen that was very impractical, but all I had to do was take one look outside the window. In a matter of minutes, I said: 'This is my apartment'."

Originally an artist's studio, built in 1840, the succession of owners had cluttered the spacious loft by building walls to section off the rooms. After Emmanuel and Andrew, an American-born classical concert pianist, acquired the apartment in 2001, they immediately set to work reconfiguring the space to suit their needs. "We didn't want the help of a decorator and decided to keep everything as open and simple as possible to remind us of the original spirit of the atelier," says Emmanuel. "What is so unusual here is that the windows face west rather than north."

Over the past eleven years, the studio has undergone three different renovations. The first step required opening the upstairs mezzanine to create a master bedroom

LEFT: The owners rebuilt the en-suite bathroom, opting for contemporary-style fittings with slate. They opened the window above the stairwell and extended the bedroom to include a space for the custom-designed closets.

RIGHT: The music room and Steinway grand piano.

with a small fireplace. At the furthest narrow strip of the mezzanine, the owners created a partially walled-in study, lined with rare books, facing the enormous floor-to-ceiling windows of the living room.

"We had to scrub and polish all the original nineteenth-century structural wooden beams. One of the former owners was reportedly a witch," says Emmanuel with a smile. "She nearly burned down the whole building and there were still charred marks on the wood." Once the former owner's unsightly carpet had been stripped away, the oak parquet floors underneath also required partial refurbishment.

After the two rooms under the stairwell were opened up, the owners renovated the bathroom with a more modern touch. The Alsatian-born conductor says that he has always loved wood and slate ("it reminds me of the family chalet of my childhood"), which determined the choice of materials of the contemporary-style sink and tub. Utilizing the new space created upstairs over the stairwell, the owners designed a wall of built-in closets, which proved to be a challenge, given the curved contour of the building. "We called in a few interior architects, then gave up and did it ourselves," says Emmanuel.

Teaming up with some of the neighbors, the owners also installed an elevator for the building, which would later figure in planning the third and most recent renovation. "We got rid of the small downstairs bathroom and extended the kitchen. Now we can use the small curved outside space on the landing to add another bathroom," Emmanuel explains. The new kitchen—a sleek-line combination of inox steel and wood—was built with practicality in mind.

ABOVE: The renovated entrance hall has a low-mirrored ceiling to give an illusion of height. "We were lucky to find an antique Chinese chest that fits exactly between the two doors of the music room," says Emmanuel.

ABOVE RIGHT AND OPPOSITE: The owners installed a fireplace in the bedroom and kept the space uncluttered and airy. The French medieval cathèdre chair and white Louis XIII armchair, made of sheep horn, are both from the family collection. Set back from the street, the bedroom is a peaceful refuge. Over the bed hangs an antique Tibetan cloth, picked up during the owners' travels. "The antique Persian rug always changes colors with the changing light," says Emmanuel.

The downstairs level of the atelier has a luminous backroom studio lined with musical scores and books, dominated by a gleaming Steinway piano, where the owners often rehearse.

To furnish the spacious airy front section of the atelier, the key concern was allowing the view of the Sacré Cœur to interact with the rest of the décor. Gilded candle sconces, found in a Parisian flea market, hang on whitewashed walls. Among the owners' eclectic antique art collection is a precious 1640 oil still life painted on wood by Pieter Claesz, a "meditation on eternity". On the opposite wall is an old, gilt-framed mercury

mirror from the Regency era that Emmanuel remembers from his childhood. "It has traveled to so many places that it is tarnished but still beautiful. You'd have to work hard to get that same effect!"

The antique furniture is a combination of acquisitions purchased during the musicians' international travels on tour and family pieces from Alsace. "My father was an architect and collected rare books that date back as early as 1684," says Emmanuel, who has kept the collection intact. Other family pieces include a signed Louis XVI chest and an antique Cuban walnut Directoire dining table. The striking seventeenth-century religious wooden statues that hang on the upstairs walls were rescued from Alsatian churches. "I remember my father taking a razor and discovering the original pigments," says Emmanuel. "In the nineteenth century, stone statues were suddenly in vogue so they were given a coat of gray paint."

"Our home is all about the space and the view," Emmanuel adds. "No matter where we travel in the world, it is always an enormous pleasure to return to Montmartre."

All of the original nineteenth-century structural wooden
beams had to be scrubbed and polished

MAISONS PAYSANNES

Though highly diverse in style, these modestly-sized homes make full use of every square foot available, combining functionality with simple uncluttered beauty. Here, the "paysanne" effect goes beyond the geographic constraint of a strictly rural dwelling, since it also implies an interactive relationship with the surrounding natural environment. This may embrace a variety of pursuits, from scouting for authentic country furnishings and linens to exploring local lime-washing techniques with split vines, hemp, and lavender. These small homes, whether situated on a remote southwestern hilltop, a strip of lush coastline, or on a tiny island in the heart of the City of Light, are imbued with unparalleled romantic intimacy.

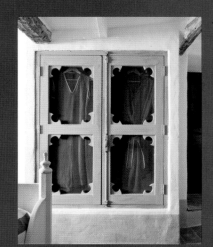

STUDIO LES LIANES
VILLEFRANCHE-SUR-MER

At the foot of a tranquil private road that winds down to the Mediterranean, the small, white Studio Les Lianes sits above a lush terraced garden of bougainvillea, oleander, wisteria, and bamboo. Partially obscured by the sun-dappled greenery and an enormous grapefruit tree, this former artist's atelier in Villefranche-sur-Mer has a one-hundred-year-old history of intertwined stories, much like the tangle of verdant creepers that cover the stone walls of the garden.

When Dutch painter Philip Zilcken and his wife, Henriette, bought this hillside parcel of land in 1914, chances are that the sweeping vista of the bay was not all that different than it is today.

Founded in fourteenth century by Charles II d'Anjou as a duty-free port, Villefranche-sur-Mer has remained surprisingly impervious to time and coastal development. The village is a maze of narrow, vaulted passageways and clusters of stacked houses, in postcard-perfect hues of dusty rose, ocher, apricot, and pale green. On the lively cobblestone quay, lined with bobbing wooden fishing boats, is the tiny fourteenth-century Chapelle St Pierre, whimsically redesigned in the 1950s by resident artist and writer, Jean Cocteau, who painted the interiors with a phantasmagorical depiction

OPPOSITE: The stonewall entrance to the Studio "Les Lianes". View of the bay of Villefranche from the garden. The shimmering Mediterranean is visible from nearly every room. Typical Provençal terra-cotta roof tiles that date back to the construction of the house in 1914.

ABOVE LEFT AND RIGHT: The sunlit dining room. The table is one of many pieces that belonged to former owner, artist Philip Zilcken. The chairs were retrieved from the family home in The Hague. The southeast-facing sea-view dining terrace, where the owners frequently entertain guests.

of the life of Saint Peter surrounded by local fishermen. Beyond la Citadelle, an imposing sixteenth-century stone fort, Les Lianes (also known as "Lianas") is located at the westernmost seaside section of Villefranche, perched above the historic military Port de la Darse where sleek mini-yachts now glide in and out of the harbor.

Over the past few decades, the villa's current owners, Helen Koch, a Dutch-born writer, and Mike Bradwell, a British theatrical director, and their daughter, Flora, a painter, have gradually refurbished their family home with a mix of Zilcken's treasure trove of furniture and paintings and weekly pilgrimages to Nice's flea market and *brocante* stores.

"The history of this house begins with my great grandmother's sister, Henrietta Selhorst, known in the family as Tajet," says Helen. "She had a lot of money and Philip Zilcken had a lot of talent." During much of his career spent in The Hague, Zilcken had achieved considerable fame as a painter of Orientalist scenes and still lifes, but he was also a multi-faceted graphic

artist, etcher, draughtsman, engraver, and lithographer. His artistic circle of friends spanned a great number of luminaries of his era: poet Paul Verlaine, writer Edmond de Goncourt, photographer Nadar, actress Sarah Bernhardt, theatrical director Lugné-Poe, sculptor Auguste Rodin, and Nabis School painters Pierre Bonnard and Edouard Vuillard.

Zilcken had discovered the dazzling pure light of Provence as early as 1882, but it was only toward the end of his career, at the age of 61, that the artist and his wife decided to leave The Hague and settle in the south of France. After a brief stay in a reportedly haunted tower of the Château of Mont-Boron in Nice, Zilcken bought a piece of land near La Darse in Villefranche. He continued to work in the peaceful gardens of his studio right up to his death, in 1930.

Once a sprawling estate, Les Lianes included a large main house (where every detail—from the window frames to a splendid curved staircase—was designed by Zilcken), the adjacent wooden atelier, and a minuscule two-leveled gatehouse where the servants slept. During the 1950s, the

OPPOSITE LEFT AND RIGHT: The owners found the turn-of-the-century wooden dresser and plates at the Nice flea market, where they frequently pick up local attic treasures. Also displayed is Zilcken's collection of pottery from Egypt and South America. The bookcase, bought at the Nice flea market, is lined with rare books and documents collected by the artist. Zilcken's armchair is placed by the window.

THIS PAGE: Helen and Mike trimmed the windows and doors with the same turquoise shade of blue that the artist originally chose for his studio.

ABOVE LEFT AND RIGHT: The French "Matisse-style" tiles and dish rack were found at flea markets. The owners, who extended the former entrance hall to create a new room, rebuilt the former tiny kitchen.

OPPOSITE LEFT AND RIGHT: "We listened to what was already there," says Helen, who conserved all of the original yellow and green floor tiles. The oak cupboard, another find at the brocante, was painted a soft gray, and is filled with a mix of dishware from local shops.

enterprising widow of a Dutch painter, Pormp Looyen, took up residence and rented out some of the rooms. As the years passed, she gradually converted Zilcken's wooden studio, a simple rustic shed, into a more liveable bungalow.

Jo Looyen-Tromp immediately added a brick fireplace for cool winter nights. "We often spent holidays with my family at Les Lianes from 1962 on. We were enamored of the place." By 1971, Bastiaan and Hilda Koch, Helen's parents, bought out the other eight heirs and acquired Zilcken's house (which was later sold), as well as the

garden atelier. Over the past forty years, this simple but enchantingly decorated family home has undergone a number of practical transformations, yet preserves the bohemian spirit of its former owner.

The family retrieved as much as possible of the smaller period furnishings from Zilcken's main house, including the round wooden dining-room table and the small desk in the sitting room, which was filled with the artist's reupholstered turn-of-the-century sofa and armchairs.

"One of the first things my mother, Hilda, did was break through the walls of the storage room, just below the house at the garden level, and make a bedroom out of the basement," Helen recalls. The owners replaced the dirt floors with checkerboard stone tiles and covered the thick walls with a coat of deep blue paint. The small bathroom, with a free-standing zinc tub that dates back to Zilcken's day, doubles as an extra bedroom, equipped with a

The owners are fond of cooking, using the freshest ingredients from the nearby local market. From this humble kitchen comes a dazzling array of regional specialties prepared by Mike Bradwell, chef extraordinaire

miniature, curved antique wrought-iron bed, found at Nice's flea market.

Enhancing the orange roof-tiled villa with a thorough whitewashing of the facade, Helen and Mike also replaced the old stone floors with polished Provençal terra-cotta tiles in the luminous southeast-facing sitting room and the adjacent sea view terrace.

Since a great deal of time and passion is devoted to cooking at Les Lianes, the most urgent challenge was to replace the antiquated postage-stamp-sized kitchen

nook in the dining room with a more modern and spacious reconfiguration. This required a partial rebuilding of the dining-room walls to create a new room at the back of the house, in the former entrance hall. The country kitchen's antique blue and white tiles ("Matisse apparently had the same ones," says Mike) were Nice flea-market finds, as are much of the vintage ceramic crockery and the gray-painted oak cupboard. To capitalize on the limited space, another renovation necessitated transforming a closet into a small but modern bathroom with a shower.

BELOW: The bedroom, at the garden level. Helen's mother, Hilda, designed the cast-iron bed in The Hague and brought it from Holland, and also put in the black and white checkerboard floor tiles. The owners repainted the whitewashed walls a deep restful blue.

RIGHT AND FAR RIGHT: An Delft plate from the family collection. The tiny bathroom and its 1900s zinc tub.

OPPOSITE RIGHT: The bathroom doubles as a modest guest room. The iron cot, from the Nice brocante, was also given a coat of blue paint.

Likewise, the former lavatory was prettily refurbished into what the owners affectionately call "the cell"—a tiny pristine bedroom with a hand-stitched white quilt draped on the single wrought-iron cot.

Much attention has been paid to preserve the simplicity and uncluttered turn-of-the-century charm of the home. Mixed with Zilcken's own treasured relics—South American pitchers, Egyptian pottery, and Japanese bric-à-brac—are many original works by the artist. The large bookcase in the sitting room is filled with Zilcken's erudite collection of tomes and a guest log, documenting the presence of his friend and neighbor, French writer Maurice Maeterlinck. A number of renowned Dutch artists were also entertained at Les Lianes, including Jan Toorop and his daughter, Charley Toorop, who is known to have painted in the lush garden.

One of the current owners' biggest surprises occurred in 2002, while cleaning out some of Zilcken's old trunks of magazines and papers in the garden storage shed. "I found a file full of old theatrical programs, and recognized one of them from the Théâtre de L'Oeuvre, run by Lugné-Poe," says Mike Bradwell. The discovery of a veritable treasure trove of original lithographs by Vuillard, Bonnard, and Toulouse-Lautrec may not be the last.

"We let the house speak to us," says Helen with a smile. As a child, she still recalls hearing rumors about the precious bounty of *objets d'art* that was hastily buried in the garden before the German Occupation. Meanwhile, Les Lianes continues to serve as a retreat from the urban "So many plays and novels have been written here by various people," Helen Koch adds. "Long may the house continue to inspire."

Tucked between the Mediterranean and the Pyrenees, the rugged remoteness of the southwestern Corbières region has a hypnotic beauty all its own. In contrast with the neighboring region of Provence, this sparsely populated area is a dramatic mix of hilltop fortressed villages with medieval Cathar castles, gently sloping river valleys, lush vineyards, and the garrigue—a rocky terrain blanketed with green scrub, fragrant wild herbs, red poppies, and yellow broom. Known for its wine, honey, and cheeses, this pocket of France is the kind of place where the population of wild boars may well outnumber the local inhabitants.

CHÂTEAU MARIANNA
CARCASSONNE

OPPOSITE: The medieval bridge in a nearby town. An undulating lime-washed wall on the small balcony. The main entrance and simple facade of what was formerly a vine grower's house. The terra-cotta ceramics were bought in a local store. A detail of a plaster-cast pillar.

ABOVE LEFT AND RIGHT: The surrounding landscape of hills that overlook the valley. With no space for a garden, the owners planted rose bushes in a wine keg in front of their village home.

Still largely uncharted territory for tourists, the wild landscape was reason enough to convince London-based designer Marianna Kennedy and her husband, Charles Gledhill, an antiquarian bookbinder, to invest in a place of their own. "We stumbled upon this house about twelve years ago while visiting our friend, artist Ian Harper, who had bought the home next door to it. You could see that the roof was caving in and I think the villagers had just forgotten about it," says Marianna.

By all accounts, different local families had lived in this modest house, then finally abandoned it. In all likelihood, the ground floor had served as a *bergerie*—a sheepfold—centuries ago. However, over time, the empty house had become more and more derelict, Marianna explains. Since it was now infringing on their friend's property and was up for sale at an affordable price, the couple decided to share the investment with London antique dealer, Peter Hone. The initial idea seemed simple enough—as far as they could tell, it was just a question of consolidating the walls and fixing the roof.

"Of course, as soon as we started to renovate the roof, we realized that absolutely everything was wrong with the house," Marianna recounts. "The beams were all

For the interior design, the owners opted for a minimalist spartan look that would maximize the elaborate artisan work done to the house

rotten and we had to re-create everything, from floors to ceilings." Teaming up with local artisan Patrick Gentil, the owners were advised to lime-render the walls with a special mix of lavender and hemp, a frequently used technique of the region. Once the insulation was finished, white plaster and casing paint were applied to the walls. "I also worked with two architects who came down from

England and we slowly brought the home back to life." To begin with, repairing the damaged terra-cotta floors was far more time-consuming than they had anticipated. "Every tile had to be scrubbed down and re-laid, one by one. Then all the doors had to be rebuilt," says the designer. Unsurprisingly, the friendly locals often dropped by, curious to see how thing were progressing. "They were

OPPOSITE: The sitting room, furnished with French provincial chairs from a local brocante. Marianna's decorative team in London made the horsehair sofa.

LEFT: Co-owner Peter Hone created all the ornamental plaster casts that hang on the walls.

ABOVE: The kitchen farm table and chairs were salvaged from the neighboring attic sales.

incredulous. They couldn't imagine what was going on in our modest little house and why it was taking so long."

Ultimately, it took five full years to finish the restoration of their tiny home, which required traveling back and forth from London to the Corbières region every six weeks. To mark its completion, the blue-shuttered stone house was baptized "Château Marianna," much to the amusement of their neighbors.

For the interior design, the owners opted for a minimalist Spartan look that would offset the elaborate artisan work done to the house. The four-level space includes a small wine cellar, a sitting room, a country-style kitchen, and a winding staircase that leads to three bedrooms and a spacious bathroom. Much of the rustic furniture was retrieved from nearby *vide-grenier* attic sales. "I've bought so many beautiful antique linens that I could open a shop," Marianna says with a smile.

ABOVE: The owners were shown a local technique using split vines on the ceiling, in between the beams, that are covered with white casing paint. The nineteenth-century wood cabinet lined with dishware is from the London antique dealer Humphrey Carrasco.

OPPOSITE: The owners opted for slate-topped counters and a stone sink that they found.

The owners were advised
to lime-render the walls with
a special mix of lavender and
hemp, a frequently used
technique of the region

OPPOSITE: The ground-floor sitting
room. Their friend and neighbor, Ian
Harper, made the geometrically
designed concrete floor.

ABOVE AND ABOVE LEFT: The
cabinets and dish rack were hand
painted in pale, natural hues.

LEFT: The desire for simplicity
extended to the dishware, found
in local shops.

ABOVE: The four-poster bed, draped with linens from the local markets, was custom-made in London and painted an electric ultramarine blue by Peter Hone.

ABOVE RIGHT AND OPPOSITE: The bathroom, with hand-painted trellis doors under the sink. "When we installed the old stone bathroom sink, the locals teased us," says Marianna. "They said it looked like something for a vache (cow) and couldn't understand why we didn't want something more modern."

All of the beds were fabricated in London by Marianna Kennedy's team, including a large four-poster in the master bedroom that the designer painted a deep shade of ultramarine blue. By deliberate choice, there are very few works of Marianna's own design. Her creations, sold at the Paris Galerie Chastel-Maréchal, range from gilded-framed mirrors and colorful hand-polished resin lamps to bronze sconces and decorative pedestal tables.

"We come down here to escape work and disconnect from London. I may draw or think about projects," Marianna says, "but it is wonderful to shut the door of your home and step into a very wild landscape. It is quiet here, even in the month of August."

The authenticity of village life—swimming in the river, wandering up to Cathar castle, or partaking in the local wild boar roasts in the evenings—contributes to the singular charm of Château Marianna. "What we find so satisfying," says Marianna, "is that now, after all that work, our house looks just as it should—as if it has always been there."

Steps away from the twelfth-century gothic landmark cathedral Notre-Dame on the Ile de la Cité, rue Chanoinesse is among the most ancient streets of Paris. Formerly part of a walled-in cloister for the ecclesiastic dignitaries of Notre-Dame, the street was not only the home of the canons—les chanoines—but also housed a number of illustrious residents throughout the centuries. Indeed, if one were to listen to the whisperings of its memory-embedded stones, nearly every building would have a tale to tell.

LA RUE CHANOINESSE

PARIS

ABOVE LEFT: Animal sculptures in bronze by owner Alexia Delrieu and a piece in black wax by Jean-Luc Parant. The armchair was salvaged from the family country house and reupholstered.

ABOVE CENTER AND RIGHT: A sunny corner of the dining room. The delicate designs on the eighteenth-century painted door depict pigeons and flower baskets filled with roses.

BELOW: The curved outer stairway. "It was beautifully designed so that the elderly ecclesiastics could climb the stairs easily," says Alexia.

OPPOSITE: The living room blends the old and new in a warm mix of colors and styles: the light fixture is from Fortuny in Venice; the bronze lamp is a creation by French sculptor Hubert Le Gall. The interchangeable coffee table covered with galusha (stingray) leather was designed by R&Y Augousti; on the wall by the original marble chimney hangs a work by Armenian artist, Davod Emdadian and an anonymous painting of a peacock with real feathers, found at the Paris flea market.

One of the most celebrated tragic love stories began here in the twelfth century, at number 10 rue Chanoinesse, when church official Canon Fulbert, uncle of a strong-willed gifted girl named Heloise, asked the brilliant teacher and philosopher Pierre Abelard to become his niece's tutor. Wishing to become better acquainted with his beautiful young student, Abelard persuaded Fulbert to allow him to move into their home. The ensuing ill-fated love affair between Abelard and Heloise and its dramatic consequences, immortalized in their famous letters, has remained an inspirational model of idealized romantic desire.

One of the darkest legends that allegedly took place in 1387 on this same street conjures the fictional character of Sweeney Todd. According to various accounts, two complicitous neighbors, a murderous barber and a pastry maker, used pieces of human flesh to prepare their own special pâté, which they sold to the inhabitants of Ile de la Cité.

Other famed French writers such as sixteenth-century poet Joachim du Bellay, and Jean Racine, a dramatic poet known for his classical tragedies, resided on a neighboring street that gave out onto rue Chanoinesse. During the twentieth century, the northern wing of a medieval *hôtel particulier* at number 12 was restored and rented to the Aga Khan and his family, who still occasionally use the townhouse when in Paris.

Ile de la Cité is one of two natural islands in the Seine, and it was the central location and spectacular river view and Notre-Dame that drew Alexia Delrieu and her family to rue Chanoinesse in 2007. An author of children's books, a part-time *bouquiniste* (seller of antique books), and a sculptor, Alexia had always lived near the river, but on the opposite bank. The idea of living on an island, she says, in the heart of the ancient quarter of Lutèce, was extremely attractive. "Most Parisian families would never think to live here because it's a very touristy area, but at the end of the day, when the tourists go home, the Ile de la Cité is like a village."

The two-story apartment is connected by a winding staircase that leads to a separate floor of cozy bedrooms for their three children: Virgile, Circé, and Tancrède. Since its former residents had

RIGHT: The living room looks out on the River Seine. The ever-changing reflections and passing barges, houseboats, and illuminated bâteaux-mouches are all part of the charm of the unique location. The trompe-l'œil wallpaper is from the Paris manufacturer Zuber.

ABOVE: On the chimneypiece, inside a nineteenth-century glass bell jar: a detail of a bridal bouquet hand-painted on a mirror.

RIGHT: The dining room exemplifies Alexia and Olivier's eclectic flair for harmony: the long dining table came from a Provençal cloth merchant; The nineteenth-century oak sloping secretary desk, rescued from the family country house, once belonged to Alexia's grandmother; the contemporary stool, designed by R&Y Augousti, is made from goat parchment and wrought iron. The drop-leaf crystal chandelier was bought at the Paris flea market. The family's beagle, Fanfare, asleep on his favorite cushions.

carefully preserved the building, it required nothing more than a fresh coat of white paint on the walls. This helped to highlight one of the most striking features—a series of delicate ornamental door paintings in the dining room that date to the eighteenth century.

All the rooms are a colorful mix of old and new, furnished with a variety of objets d'art that Alexia and her husband, Olivier, a business executive, bring back from their travels. "We have a passion for Italy. Every time we return, we always buy fabric and hanging lamps from the same little boutiques we discovered in Venice years ago."

Much of the furniture in the living room and adjacent dining room was hand-picked by Alexia, who has worked as an auctioneer in Aix-en-Provence. "It was great training to see what people are

buying," she says. One of her finds from Provence is a cloth merchant's long, narrow wooden table that formerly served to unspool fabrics or fold sheets. It is used for everything from a practical workspace to an elegantly set candlelit dinner. A more contemporary piece is a three-part movable coffee table covered with galusha (stingray) leather by designer R&Y Augousti, set in front of the living room sofa. "The nineteenth-century squat *crapaud* armchairs came from my grandmother's country house," says Alexia, who reupholstered them with bold-patterned fabrics. "I was also lucky to have a great-grandmother who was an artist." Her drawings, also retrieved from the country home, are now framed in the master bedroom. A number of other paintings that hang on the walls were acquired at auctions at Drouot, such as the impressive sixteenth-century oil by a Flemish master portraying Apollo and Venus. Alexia's own bronze animal sculptures are on display in the living room, sitting atop two ancient Syrian wooden trunks from Olivier's family collection.

OPPOSITE LEFT: A glimpse of the Notre-Dame Cathedral from the kitchen, "an ideal view of Paris".

OPPOSITE RIGHT: The simple kitchen is a showcase for the children's impressive butterfly collection.

BELOW: The master bedroom, which may have once served as the kitchen, features an antique black and white faience wood stove which doubles up as a shelf for Alexia's angel sculpture, seashells, and coral.

RIGHT: The bedroom is a mix of finds picked up during the family's frequent trips, such as the Turkish embroidered bedspread and kangaroo-skin rugs. On the wall behind the bed hangs a photo by Jean-Baptiste Huynh.

The originality of this home lies in its artful balance of disparate styles, textures, and colors within a limited space. Above all, this harmonious blend—furniture rescued from the family attics or *brocante* markets, original and antique artwork, travel mementos, and contemporary pieces—is offset by the privileged urban vista of sky and water. "The river is very animated—the passing houseboats, the illuminated *bateaux-mouches*, the fishermen, the firemen doing their exercises at the edge of the bank, the ducks, the swans—there is always something happening," says Alexia. "We're constantly lulled by the rhythms of Notre-Dame—the cathedral bells toll every fifteen minutes!"

INDEX

ACKNOWLEDGMENTS

Lanie Goodman, Simon Brown, and CICO Books would like to thank all the home owners who
so generously opened their homes to us. Their kindness and hospitality are much appreciated.

CHÂTEAU DE OUTRELAISE, pages 20–35:
www.outrelaise.com

CHÂTEAU DE TOCQUEVILLE, pages 36–51:
www.chateaudetocqueville.com

SAVOYARD CHALET, pages 54–67:
www.sibuethotels-spa.com

LES CONFINES, pages 68–79: Dominique
and Bruno Lafourcade's private property
in Provence. The couple designed the
architecture and garden themselves.
www.architecture-lafourcade.com,
www.dominique-lafourcade.com

VILLA BAULIEU, pages 90–103: The
Guénant family designed and restored the
Villa Baulieu in collaboration with a team
of painters, decorators, and craftsmen.
Among them are architect and interior
decorator Guy-Marie Kieffer, and Provençal
fireplace gypseries by Pierre Caron.

LOU MAZET DE L'ESTAGNET, pages
106–117: Viviane Vidal de la Blache's
exclusive women's fashion boutique
Bla-Bla, Place Garonne, 83990 St Tropez
(+33 4 94 97 45 09)

ARTIST'S ATELIER, pages 118–127:
www.joyderohanchabot.com

LA MAISON DU BONHEUR, pages 128–137:
architect: Amine Klam
painter-decorator: Roberto Bergero
gardener: www.lesfleursdubien.fr

CHÂTEAU MARIANNA, pages 158–167:
www.mariannakennedy.com

For their generous advice and support,
the author would like thank the following:
Andrée Lotey-Goodman, Judy Fayard,
Alexander Lobrano, Norma Brown-Hill,
Laure Jakobiak, Melanie Fleishman, Beverly
Pimsleur, Adam Redolfi, and Michel Redolfi.